An Advent Journey

An Advent Journey
Preparing the Way of the Lord
Larry R. Kalajainen

AN ADVENT JOURNEY
Copyright © 1993 by Larry R. Kalajainen
All rights reserved.

No part of this book may be reproduced in any manner whatsoever without written permission except in the case of brief quotations embodied in critical articles or reviews. For information, address THE UPPER ROOM, 1908 Grand Avenue, Post Office Box 189, Nashville, Tennessee 37202-0189.

Unless otherwise designated, scripture quotations are from the *New Revised Standard Version*, copyright © 1989 by the Division of Christian Education of the National Council of Churches of Christ in the United States of America, and are used by permission.

Scripture quotations designated JB are from *The Jerusalem Bible*, copyright © 1966 by Darton, Longman, & Co., Inc.

KJV is used to identify quotations from the King James Version of the Bible.

The publisher gratefully acknowledges permission to reprint the following copyrighted material:

"O Come, O Come, Emmanuel" sts. 1, 3, 5ab, 6cd, 7ab from *The Hymnal 1940*, © 1943, renewed 1981 The Church Hymnal Fund; trans. sts. 4, 5cd, 6ab, 7cd © 1989 The United Methodist Publishing House. Reprinted from *The United Methodist Hymnal* by permission.

Prayers for Days 8 and 15 are from *The Fathers of the Church*, Vols. 71 & 75 and are used by permission of the Catholic University of America Press.

Prayers for Days 10, 17–21 are from *Early Christian Prayers* edited by A. Hamman and translated by Walter Mitchell. Copyright © 1961 by Regnery Gateway. Reprinted by special permission of Regnery Gateway, Inc.

While every effort has been made to secure permission, we may have failed in a few cases to trace or contact the copyright holder. We apologize for any inadvertent oversight or error.

Cover design: Jim Bateman
Printed in the United States of America
First printing: August 1993 (15)
ISBN: 0-8358-0690-1

DEDICATION

Every book has more than one author. Spouses, children, friends, colleagues, and a host of others provide inspiration, insight, and valuable constructive criticism. It would be impossible to name all those who have contributed in some way to this book. I owe special thanks to my wife, Carol, who has offered unstinting support as well as wise critical analysis. David Cousins, colleague, mentor, and friend, read some of the early pages and gave his usual thorough and pertinent comments. I also want to express my gratitude to those members of the United Methodist Church at New Brunswick who not only encouraged their pastor to write but actually volunteered to "test drive" a draft of the manuscript during Advent, 1992, and offered many valuable suggestions for improvement. Thanks also to the members of The First United Methodist Church of Westfield, NJ, who tested the draft version.

*I affectionately dedicate this book
to all of these persons,
journeying in the life of the Spirit.*

CONTENTS

Introduction ✳ 9

How to Use This Book ✳ 14

Introductory Group Meeting ✳ 15

Week One: The Coming One ✳ 17
Day 1 – Day 7 ✳ 19–41
Readings from the Gospel of Mark
Group Meeting for Week One ✳ 42

Week Two: The Anointed One ✳ 45
Day 8 – Day 14 ✳ 47–67
Readings from the Gospel of Matthew
Group Meeting for Week Two ✳ 68

Week Three: The Savior ✳ 71
Day 15 – Day 21 ✳ 72–95
Readings from the Gospel of Luke
Group Meeting for Week Three ✳ 96

Week Four: The Word ✳ 99
Day 22 – Day 29 ✳ 101–127
Readings from the Gospel of John
Group Meeting for Week Four ✳ 128

INTRODUCTION

While much of the world waits for the stroke of midnight on December 31 to usher in a new year, Christians keep time by a different calendar. For us, New Year's Day always occurs on a Sunday—the first Sunday of Advent. Christians are not the only ones who keep time to the rhythms of their religious feasts or sacred events. Jews and Muslims also mark time, not only by the movements of the planets and stars but by sacred story. Just as the solar or lunar calendar provides a regularity to life and enables us to measure intervals, so the liturgical calendar helps us order our life in time. It is not so much a way of measuring time as it is a way of living in time. We observe the seasons of the gospel as a way of ordering our lives according to the gospel.

The gospel is a proclamation about the saving acts of God and the sovereign rule of God over the creation, revealed in the person of Jesus of Nazareth. The birth, life, ministry, death, and resurrection of Jesus are at the heart of the Christian faith. Without Jesus, there is no Christian faith. So it is natural that the interpretations of Jesus in the Gospels of our New Testament hold such a central place in our understanding of ourselves and of our place in the world. The gospel seasons—Advent, Christmas, Epiphany, Lent, Easter, and Pentecost—come from these stories. Christians mark the two most theologically significant events of Jesus' life, his birth and resurrection, with the two major feasts of the Christian year, Christmas and Easter. The other seasons (or "feasts" to use the traditional language) derive their significance from the two major ones.

The Scriptures portray both Jesus' birth and his resurrection from the dead as the result of God's creative acts. The power of the Holy Spirit comes upon Mary, and she conceives a new life. The life-giving power of God invades the domain of death and the crucified Messiah lives again.

Advent is a season of preparation for the Feast of the Nativity. At the feast of Jesus' baptism (Epiphany), he receives his vocation, and his ministry follows. This ministry has universal dimensions and scope, symbolized by the story of the Gentile Magi who come to pay homage to the newborn Messiah. Lent heralds the approach of Easter and culminates in the story of Jesus' sufferings during Holy Week. Easter has the power to color even the horrors of the passion. The day of crucifixion becomes Good Friday in light of Easter. An ugly execution has saving power because of his resurrection from the dead. Jesus' ascension to the throne of lordship likewise follows upon resurrection; and the ascension, in turn, makes possible the descent of the Spirit upon the community of Jesus' followers, which we celebrate at Pentecost.

The movement of the gospel seasons tells us that time itself has become sacred because the mighty acts of God in Jesus Christ have invaded it. For the believer, time is no longer merely the ticks of the clock or the pages of a calendar. Time has a quality and significance beyond duration. It has a certain feel and texture. It is no longer just *chronos*—clock time. It is *kairos*—the right time, the fulfillment of time. Living to the rhythm of the gospel seasons keeps our inner life tuned to *kairos* time rather than *chronos* time.

If the Feast of the Nativity (Christmas) is the first of the major gospel feasts, why do we begin the year with Advent? It was not always so. However, by the late fourth century, the church had instituted Lent as a period of preparation for the celebration of Easter, the Feast of the Resurrection of Christ. Because Holy Week, which commemorates Jesus' passion, preceded Easter, Lent naturally took on an extremely somber tone. After all, our sin nailed Jesus to the cross. So the penitential tone of Lent, which was expressed by strict fasting and self-denial, was the appropriate mood for contemplation of Christ's sufferings and our participation and culpability in them.

With Lent as a model, the church developed Advent as a comparable period of preparation for the Feast of the Nativity, or Christmas. The practice of a period of preparation for Christmas probably began in the fifth century, although the existing Advent liturgies are from the sixth century. The idea of Advent appears to have originated in Gaul, which corresponded roughly to modern-day France. Though the length of Advent varied considerably in the early days, the Western church eventually settled on a period of four Sundays prior to December 25, which was the date in the West for celebrating Jesus' birth. In the Eastern church, which celebrates Christmas on Epiphany, the length of Advent has continued to correspond to that of Lent, or approximately six weeks, beginning in mid-November.

The word *advent* derives from the Latin root meaning "to come" or "to arrive." The Feast of Christ's Nativity always has had something of a dual focus on both the joyous first coming of Jesus as Emmanuel—God is with us—and on his second advent as returning Lord and Judge. So the mood of the season has been sober but not somber like Lent. An emphasis on expectation and hope accompanies the note of penitence. Fasting and other forms of self-denial have not been as strict as those in Lent, though Advent has retained the penitential color of purple.

The human experience that Advent symbolizes is the experience of waiting. In the modern world, we usually view waiting as a bad thing. We want instant gratification. When we need something, we need it yesterday. When we're going somewhere, we want to be there now. In our visually oriented society, a picture is not only worth a thousand words; it's worth a thousand minutes of the time it would take us to study or read. Sound bites become substitutes for critical thought. Microwave ovens cut down the waiting time, as well as much of the flavor, of our meals. Recent years have seen a steady decrease in the number of people who are learning to play musical instruments. It takes too long to learn, too much time spent in the hard disciplines of practice. Who wants to spend the years necessary to make a violin produce a sound of heavenly sweetness rather than the hellish squawks it produces in the hands of a beginner?

Yet waiting belongs to the very nature of human existence. We enter life after a prolonged period of gestation, and we exit life after waiting for our hearts to stop beating. And in between our birth and our death are many more experiences of waiting—days, months, even years when our lives seem to be "on hold." What makes waiting so difficult is that while we are waiting we feel that we are not in control. Someone or something else is controlling the pace and content of our lives. The experience of not being in control is fearful. It unsettles us, disturbs us, makes us afraid. However, if we are at all reflective, we would admit that we are hardly ever in control. The sense of being in control is really an illusion. Much of our activity, our busy-ness, and our frustration with waiting stems from our desire to maintain the illusion that we are in control of our lives.

Advent is the season that gives voice to this common human experience of waiting. This season gives us an opportunity to discover, not how we can escape waiting, but how can we wait so that the waiting itself becomes a means of grace. Just as Mary and Joseph waited for the birth of their baby, and Simeon and Anna waited for the revelation of God's deliverance, so we wait for the consummation of that deliverance at the Second Advent of Christ. Our celebration of Christmas, the first Advent, is meaningful because we are awaiting the Second. What we anticipate in the future makes the celebration of the past full of promise and hope.

❋ ❋ ❋ ❋ ❋

I have designed this series of spiritual exercises for Advent to help all of us learn to wait actively, with hope and anticipation. Beginning with the first Sunday in Advent, each week will focus on scriptures from one of the four Gospels. The scriptures were chosen for their appropriateness to the dual focus on both the first and second advents of Christ. I chose to begin the study with Mark for two reasons: First, the texts from Mark, which particularly emphasize the second advent of Christ, are those that appear in the Sunday lectionaries at the beginning of the Advent season. Second, this order places the birth narratives of Matthew and Luke closer to Christmas.

The headings for each week are significant ways of understanding Jesus, which each of the four evangelists expresses in his Gospel. The scripture notes give textual and contextual background to help the reader "get into" the passage more fully. The "Living into the Text" sections provide a series of questions designed to help the reader focus on the scripture in a personal and contemplative way. Used in this manner, the scriptures become a mirror, or a window, enabling us to see ourselves in our relationship to God more clearly.

The "Living out of the Text" component offers suggestions for moving from the inward journey to the outward journey, from contemplation of the inner self to contemplation of the self in relationship to the world outside. The Christian life, while deeply and intimately personal, is never private. It is always life-in-relationship, and the Christian life involves all our relationships—relationships to God, to self, to others, and to social structures. The gospel of Jesus Christ is a public proclamation about what is true for the whole creation. So while the suggestions for inner reflection are necessarily more numerous, they are not more important than the suggestions for the journey into the more public world of relationships that engages us all.

Each day's reading begins with "Preparation," which includes prayers from early Christian leaders and teachers. All prayers, except as noted on the copyright page, are taken from *Earliest Christian Prayers*, edited by F. Forrester Church and Terrence J. Mulry (New York: Macmillan; London: Collier Macmillan, 1988). These prayers connect us to our spiritual ancestors, pioneers in the spiritual journey before us. Apart from the ninth-century Advent Antiphons (all of which are taken from *Meditations on the O Antiphons*, The O Antiphons Text: The Sisters of St. Benedict; The Liturgical Press; Collegeville, MN 56301) used during the first week and the Leonine Sacramentary used in the final group meeting, all the prayers are prayers by individuals. With the exception of the Antiphons, all come from the first four centuries of the church. All of us learn to pray by following models. I hope that these exemplary models will teach us all to be better pray-ers.

Several persons who tested an early draft of this study expressed some initial surprise that it was not more "Christmas-y." As one person put it, "I was expecting inspirational thoughts on how hard it was for poor Mary to ride the donkey to Bethlehem, and how sad Joseph and Mary felt when they were turned away from the inn." I hope this study will provide spiritual preparation for a deeper and more meaningful celebration of Christmas, but it is not a Christmas study. It is an Advent study. The emphasis is on themes appropriate to Advent—despair and hope, disappointment and anticipation, repentance and transformation. The goal is that when we come to the celebration of the nativity of Christ, we will come as different people, as those who have heard and heeded the herald's message, "Prepare the way of the Lord, make his paths straight" (Mark 1:3).

I also hope that during this Advent journey, your own mind and heart will be caught up in the expectation and hope that is the mood of this first season of the Christian New Year. The world desperately needs to see a community of people who live in hope rather than in despair. Learning to keep time by the rhythms of the gospel seasons is one avenue by which hope may enter our lives. As you meditate on scripture, pray, sing, and repent, may you find your heart lifted up to join the expression of the earliest Christians. It was both a shout of hope and a cry for deliverance: "Maranatha!" Our Lord, come!

Larry R. Kalajainen
Epiphany, 1993
New Brunswick, NJ

HOW TO USE THIS BOOK

The format of the book assumes that regular communion with God through prayer, meditation on scripture, and inward reflection is absolutely indispensable to growth in the Christian life. We must have communion with God if we are to become spiritually mature in faith, hope, and love.

Individual Use

However, not everyone is at the same place on the spiritual journey. All of us are beginners and will always be, but some have been beginning longer than others. Some may find it possible to consider all of the reflection questions every day, while others may find it possible to do only one or two. *Not everything in every exercise is for everyone every day.* Take this journey at your own pace. The book is for you. You are not bound to the book. Use the offered resources in the way best suited to your own needs. Do not allow the self-imposed pressure to finish each day's exercise to become another source of guilt or frustration. We all have enough of those already.

Because the day of the week on which Christmas falls varies from year to year, the last week of exercises has a flexible design. Use the scripture lesson John 1:14-18 for Christmas Day, regardless of the day of the week on which it falls.

Group Use

I have provided suggestions for a group exercise for each week of the Advent journey. If you are using this book as part of a group study at your church or in your faith community, do not feel bound to the suggestions for group discussion. Use only what is useful.

Journal Keeping

The workbook format allows some space for writing your thoughts, reflections, and prayers as you go through the daily exercises. For more extensive writing, you may choose to purchase a notebook of some kind. Keeping a journal is an important tool for spiritual growth. It is much easier to get our feelings out where we can look at them when we write them down. So I encourage you to try keeping a journal through this Advent journey. Writing daily as you work through these exercises is one way to develop a helpful discipline. Anything and everything is grist for your journal—feelings, insights, questions, reactions to readings and prayers. Looking back over what you've written several months, or even years earlier, will give you a much clearer picture of where you've been, how far you've come, and perhaps indicate where you're going.

INTRODUCTORY

Group Meeting

To the Convener:

Hold an initial group meeting prior to the start of Advent. This meeting will allow participants to become familiar with the book, to read the introduction, to begin to know the others in the group, and to be prepared to begin the individual exercises on the first Sunday of Advent. Limit group size to no more than twelve people. If more than twelve people wish to participate, form smaller groups.

* Arrange chairs in a circle or sit around a table to create an atmosphere of intimacy conducive to open sharing.
* Begin or end the first group meeting with a short devotion. In subsequent weeks, other members of the group may volunteer or be asked to lead in devotions.
* Provide name tags for participants. If group participants do not know one another, plan some "getting to know you" activities.

Procedure

1. Begin with a brief devotion, led by the convener. The devotions may involve group participation.

2. Spend some time getting acquainted, particularly if the group members do not know one another very well. Don't just get names, however. Be ready to share something about yourself—where you live, where you work, your hobby, and so forth. The point is to begin establishing a tone where sharing with one another is comfortable.

3. Ask group members to take several minutes and silently read the portion of the Introduction that tells about Advent (pp. 9–11). Then spend a short time in discussion:

   What does this brief section tell you that you didn't know before?

   In what personal ways have you observed Advent, other than participation in church activities?

Have you used an Advent wreath in your home? What family traditions do you observe?

In what ways do you feel the need for a season of spiritual preparation before Christmas?

4. Share your reasons for participating in this Advent journey. Then ask: What are you hoping to get from it? help in learning to pray? a chance to study scripture in a contemplative way? a desire to know God more deeply? an escape from the commercialism of this season so that you can really celebrate Christmas for what it is?

If group members are uncomfortable sharing, don't pressure them. But part of growth in faith and love as a Christian involves opening up to others and allowing them to open up to you. Don't back away from personal sharing too quickly. Continue sharing until a natural winding down to silence occurs. Don't rush to fill up gaps with talking. Begin to listen to the silences.

5. Pass out the study books when the sharing time winds down. Walk the group members through the format. Be sure to stress that a regular and disciplined use of the daily exercises is an important component of the study. A major part of the purpose of the study is to help Christians form holy habits of daily prayer and reflection on scripture.

Do not allow this daily routine to become a source of pressure or anxiety. If one misses a daily exercise, do not do two exercises the next day. A too-casual approach, where one uses the book in a hit-or-miss fashion, will defeat the purpose and bring little benefit. A too-rigorous approach will bring feelings of guilt at failure, likewise defeating the purpose of drawing the participant into a deeper and freer walk with God.

Indicate also that not everyone will find it possible or desirable to cover all the material in each daily lesson. For some persons, one reflection question will occupy the allotted study time. The point is *not to do everything* but *to do something every day* if possible. At the very least, read the scripture passage along with the explanatory notes. Then, even when engaged in other activities through the day, reflection may take place.

6. Answer any questions related to the use of the material or the study itself. Announce the time and place of the next meeting. If possible, meet on the last day of each week or the first day of the next. The Sundays in Advent are the most appropriate time, but this time slot is not the only possibility.

7. Close by observing some moments of silence and then say the Lord's Prayer together.

WEEK ONE

THE COMING ONE

We often call the first three Gospels in our New Testament, Matthew, Mark, and Luke, the Synoptic Gospels—not only because they contain many of the same stories, sayings, and traditions about Jesus, but also because they show evidence of literary interdependence. More than 150 years of modern historical and scientific research on these three Gospels has led to the nearly unanimous conclusion that Mark was the earliest written New Testament Gospel and that both Matthew and Luke used Mark's Gospel as one of their sources.

The Gospel of Mark is much shorter than either Matthew or Luke; it includes no traditions about the origin or birth of Jesus. For many centuries, the church gave this Gospel short shrift because of its brevity and seemingly artless style. But in recent years, students of the Gospels have come to realize that Mark is a work of great theological subtlety and literary sophistication.

Many surprises await the careful reader. For instance, Mark begins his work with a title, or superscription, that immediately signals his agenda: "The beginning of the good news of Jesus Christ, the Son of God."[1] We have a clear idea of Mark's understanding of Jesus: Jesus is the Son of God, and his story is good news.

Yet in Mark's story, the only affirmations of Jesus' identity as Son of God come from 1) the heavenly voice at his baptism and at the transfiguration, 2) demons that Jesus exorcises, and 3) a Roman centurion who helped crucify him. Never does this designation appear on the lips of Jesus' family or his disciples. In fact, his disciples display an incredible obtuseness, and his family members want to lock him up because they think he's gone mad. Scripture students now recognize these surprises, which are only a few awaiting the careful reader, as themes Mark has introduced in order to convey his message about Jesus to the Christian community of which he was a part.

Chapter 13, which consists of a collection of sayings attributed to Jesus, provides a window through which we may glimpse Mark's community and some of his special concerns. This chapter is perplexing in many ways. It interweaves sayings that warn of an imminent historical disaster in which Jerusalem will be destroyed and people will have to flee to the mountains for safety with other sayings about the coming of the Son of Adam[2] at the end of the age, when the angels will gather the elect and destroy the wicked. Such apocalyptic[3] language is characteristic of a community that is feeling pressured and threatened, either by persecution from religious and political authorities or by ostracism from the mainstream of Christianity. The more alienated any community of people is from the dominant value systems and structures that surround it, the more likely that the community will take comfort in visions of the End.

Many scholars see the literary motif of the disciples' blindness and their persistent failure to understand who Jesus was, as evidence that Mark's community was a sectarian group, alienated from the mainstream church where the disciples of Jesus were heroic figures and the leading authorities. For others, the apocalyptic language of this chapter indicates that Mark's community was predominantly Jewish Christians who were experiencing sharp conflict within their families and within their social and religious networks.

Whatever chapter 13 may tell us about Mark's community, it shows us a community in an expectant posture of waiting for the consummation of the present age. As such, it becomes an appropriate entry point into the season of Advent. All of us can identify with the feelings of social alienation that permeate this chapter. At times, which of us hasn't felt that society is out of control and we long for something or someone to come and put it right? At times, which of us hasn't faced problems so overwhelming that we felt like "fleeing to the mountains"? In certain moments of stress or anxiety, which of us hasn't felt like crying, "How long, O Lord, . . . how long?" Mark 13 gives voice to those feelings of alienation, frustration, longing, and hope that all of us share and explore in this season of Advent.

---

[1] In some ancient manuscripts, the words *Son of God* do not appear in Mark 1:1, and some scholars do not give them any weight. My own view is that though the textual evidence is ambiguous, what Mark does with that title is not. For him it is a major literary theme that works itself out along the lines I have described. Whether he put it in his superscription or whether it was added later by someone who understood its significance for Mark's agenda, it remains true that the identification of Jesus as Son of God is left to a heavenly voice, demons, and one of Jesus' executioners.

[2] I have rendered the Greek phrase *ton huion tou anthropou* (literally, the son of man) as Son of Adam because the Greek word *anthropos* is the generic word for human being. *Anthropos* is a translation of the Hebrew word *adam*, which is also the generic word for human being.

[3] The word *apocalyptic* refers to a mind-set or worldview that sees the present as hopelessly in the grip of evil forces. Persons with this mind-set project hope forward to an idealized future brought into being by divine intervention and judgment. They use "end of the world" language and fantastic visions to describe this perfect future.

DAY 1

PREPARING THE WAY OF THE LORD

Preparation

Each day, as you begin these exercises, take a few moments to prepare yourself for your journey with God. It may help you to be more focused if you choose a particular spot—a favorite room or a favorite chair. Let that be your special place for meeting God. Some people find it useful to look steadily at an icon, a cross, a candle, or some other religious symbol as a way of freeing themselves from concerns of the day's work, chores awaiting attention, or relationships with other people. To help center yourself, take a few moments to quietly relax with some deep breathing. The use of visual aids or a short prayer or phrase from scripture repeated silently will help you become present both to yourself and to the Lord. Spiritual guides in the Eastern Orthodox tradition call this centering of one's inner attention "descending with the mind into the heart." What a beautiful and appropriate expression!

When you have spent a few moments in silent centering, pray the following prayer from the Advent Antiphons, an ancient liturgy from the ninth century:

> *O Emmanuel, our King and Lawgiver,*
> *The Expected of the nations and their Savior,*
> *Come and save us, O Lord, our God.*

You may also wish to sing or hum the first verse of "O Come, O Come Emmanuel," which is based on the Advent Antiphons:

> *O come, O come, Emmanuel,*
> *and ransom captive Israel,*
> *that mourns in lonely exile here*
> *until the Son of God appear.*
> *Rejoice! Rejoice! Emmanuel shall come*
> *to thee, O Israel.*

Scripture: Read Mark 1:1-11.

The opening statement of Mark's Gospel is more than a title, though it serves that function. It also states up front Mark's understanding of Jesus and of his project of telling the story of Jesus. Whatever else Mark knows or believes, he believes Jesus to be "the Son of God" (though what that means for Mark may be something radically different from popular understanding). He also believes that his story about Jesus is "good news."

As did most of the New Testament writers, Mark read the Hebrew scriptures through the lens of the church's experience of Jesus and his story. Verse 2 is a citation from Malachi 3:1, and verse 3 is a citation from Isaiah 40:3. The fact that Mark attributes both verses to Isaiah is consistent with someone's recalling a quote from memory rather than actually looking it up and writing it down.

By placing the quotation at the beginning of his narrative of John's ministry, Mark interprets that ministry as one of preparation for the coming of the Son of God and connects it to the work of the great Israelite prophets. Just as the prophets called God's people to repentance, so now John calls them to repent and prepare for something or Someone who is coming. John contrasts the baptism that he administers with that which the Coming One will administer—the baptism with the Holy Spirit.

Mark then tells us that Jesus at his own baptism by John sees a vision of the heavens torn open and the Spirit descending upon him. A heavenly voice accompanying this descent affirms what Mark has told us already—that Jesus is God's Son, the Beloved.

Living into the Text

The quotation from Isaiah, "Prepare the way of the Lord, make his paths straight," conjures up the image of an ancient monarch, who intends to pay a royal visit to his far-flung domains. Months ahead of time, he sends out heralds and a corps of royal engineers to prepare the roads on which he is to travel. They clear away fallen rocks and trees, fill in ruts and potholes, and smooth over rough spots. How is the repentance that John called for like the preparations made by the corps of engineers? What are the ruts and potholes, the rough places, the fallen rocks and trees in your life that need clearing away in order for you to be prepared for the coming of the Royal One?

It's not enough merely to identify the places in our lives where repentance is needed; we must actually repent—actually do the clearing away and the filling in and the smoothing over. What specific action will you need to take in order to carry out your repentance? an apology to someone you've hurt or wronged? a change of habitual selfish behavior? seeking professional help for addictive or compulsive behavior? setting different priorities and goals for your life?

What would it mean for you to be baptized with the Holy Spirit? Think about this question in behavioral terms rather than doctrinal or theological terms. How would your present way of life and behavior change if the Coming One who baptizes with the Holy Spirit visited you? Be as concrete as you can.

Ask the Lord to give you the courage to repent of whatever is preventing you from experiencing what you have envisioned your life could be like if Christ were to baptize you with the Holy Spirit. Close your reflection with a few moments of silent prayer.

Living out of the Text

Begin your Advent preparation by choosing one area of your life—a relationship in which you're involved, a situation in which you feel trapped, a compulsion that has you in its grip—and take some appropriate action. In other words, *begin* to repent. Repentance is not a one-time, all-at-once action. Repentance must become a way of life, so that we are always preparing the way of the Lord. Don't think you have to do it all this very moment. You couldn't, even if you tried. But begin. You may not be able to do everything that needs doing but do something.

Since today is Sunday, make a special effort to be present in worship with your faith community. The discipline of regular corporate worship is an essential ingredient in spiritual growth. If you're doing this meditation after worship has ended, reflect on your experience of worship today. Was God truly praised in your community? Did you fully enter into that corporate praise? What word from God, if any, did you hear?

DAY 2

PROCLAIMING THE GOOD NEWS OF GOD

Preparation

Pray this prayer from the Advent Antiphons:

*O Wisdom, who came forth from
the mouth of the Most High,
reaching from end to end,
and ordering all things mightily and sweetly:
Come, and teach us the way of prudence.*

Spend a few moments centering yourself by reflecting on Jesus as the Wisdom of God. Imagine that the Divine Wisdom is bringing order to your own chaotic inner self. Again, you may wish to hum or sing the second stanza of "O Come, O Come Emmanuel":

*O come, thou Wisdom from on high,
and order all things far and nigh;
to us the path of knowledge show
and cause us in her ways to go.
Rejoice! Rejoice! Emmanuel shall
come to thee, O Israel.*

Scripture: Read Mark 1:12-15.

In Mark's story, a time of testing in the wilderness immediately follows Jesus' reception of his vocation at his baptism. However, Mark tells us little about this time of testing, except that Jesus was in the company of the wild beasts and that angels cared for him. Possibly Mark is alluding to the story of Israel's time in the wilderness following the Exodus, a time also characterized by testing and God's provision of manna.

Though he will not tell us about John's arrest until chapter 6, Mark mentions it here as the precipitating event for the beginning of Jesus' own public ministry in Galilee. The one preparing the way is now out of the way, and the one whose coming he announced comes with an announcement of his own. Verse 15 is Mark's summary of the content of Jesus' ministry and teaching, distilled to its very essence. It is a signal to the reader that Mark interprets the ministry of Jesus as the place where the reign of God intersects with human history. If Jesus' life and ministry marks that intersection, then the only appropriate response is repentance and faith.

Living into the Text

Think back to a time in your life when you felt a special clarity about what you were to do, about the direction your life was to take. In what ways did you have a sense of being tested? Try to recall the feelings of that time of testing. How were you aware of the ministry of the "angels"? Who were the angels for you? How did the time of testing sharpen or dull your sense of clarity about your life and vocation? You may want to use the space below or your journal to record your thoughts. You may be going through such an experience now. If so, try to describe it as fully as you can.

The phrase usually translated as "the kingdom of God" does not refer primarily to a place but rather to a mode of existence; it means human life lived under the reign or imperial rule of God. To Mark's community, living under Roman imperial rule, this "kingdom of God" would have had political as well as personal overtones.

Under whose reign or rule do you live? What or who is the sovereign power in your life? One way to answer this question might be to look at your calendar or appointment book. What or who has the highest claim on your time? Another way to assess claims on your life might be to look at your checkbook or credit card statements. What does your pattern of spending tell you about what or who exercises sovereignty over you? Are the powers under whose rule you currently live ones that liberate and give joy or ones that enslave and burden you?

We cannot ignore the political dimension either. Whose rule does the Christian community recognize as having the ultimate claim or allegiance?

If God really were sovereign in your life, would this be "good news" to you? Why or why not? What specifically would change if God were the sovereign power in your life? The answer to this question will pinpoint the area of your life that needs repentance and faith.

Close this time of reflection by praying the Lord's Prayer. As you pray the petition, "Thy kingdom come," mentally substitute "May your sovereign rule come, may your will be done on earth." Notice how the prayer takes on a different meaning.

Living out of the Text

Since human life is always lived in social relationships, we can never confine the good news of God's reign to a personal or private matter. The prayer for God's sovereign rule to come on earth is a prayer that encompasses personal, social, and political relationships. Begin to look at your own social relationships—with family, friends, colleagues, classmates—and try to see how those relationships could be different if God's sovereignty were the energizing power within each of them. Look around you at the larger community where you live and work. Where in the public arena does the "good news" of God's reign need proclamation, and how could you become the proclaimer?

DAY 3

THE BEGINNING OF THE END

Preparation

Sit quietly in a relaxed position, and meditate for a few moments on this third stanza of the Advent Antiphons:

*O Adonai and Leader of the house of Israel,
who appeared to Moses in the flames of the bush
and gave him the law on Sinai:
Come, and with your outstretched arm redeem us.*

Pray for God's presence to be as real for you as it was for Moses when he stood before the burning bush and heard the thunder on Mount Sinai. Then hum or sing softly the stanza of "O Come, O Come Emmanuel" that corresponds to this antiphon:

*O come, O come, great Lord of might,
who to thy tribes on Sinai's height
in ancient times once gave the law
in cloud and majesty and awe.
Rejoice! Rejoice! Emmanuel shall
come to thee, O Israel.*

Scripture: Read Mark 13:1-8.

This chapter is difficult to interpret for at least two reasons. First, it is necessary to understand that among the many variations of Jewish religious thought and practice current at the time of Jesus and the earliest Christians were groups characterized by an "apocalyptic" outlook. These forms of Judaism arose several hundred years earlier than Jesus' time.

Historical catastrophes, the experience of defeat by enemies, the decline of religious observance, and a feeling that society was "going to the dogs," gave rise in some circles of Judaism to a mood of pessimism regarding the possibility of God's rule becoming a reality in the present historical order. Life in the present was understood to be dominated by evil powers, both natural and supernatural. Hope for the realization of God's rule was projected beyond the present world to a future age of blessedness that would begin when God acted decisively to end the present age of wickedness and destroy the evil powers. Some pious Jews believed that this transition from the present evil age to the future blessed age would take place when the messiah came. These people may have been the ones most ready to accept Jesus as the messiah, believing that with his coming the dawn of the future age of blessing was at hand.

This particular strain of thought within Judaism gave rise to a genre of literature that often presented interpretations of current events as though they were the predictions of long-dead heroes, which had recently been discovered. These books were called apocalypses, which means "revealing" or "revelation," and they often were ascribed to an ancient hero. Many of them use fantastic and even grotesque imagery to convey their message (such as beasts with seven heads and ten horns, angels opening books with seven seals and unleashing various plagues). However, the message itself and the worldview behind it—rather than the literary form or imagery—are what determine whether a writing is apocalyptic. The writers' purpose was to give hope to people who were experiencing tough times.

The Book of Daniel and parts of several of the prophetic books (Ezekiel and Zechariah) are examples of apocalyptic literature. In the New Testament, the Book of Revelation is the prime example. Mark 13 and its parallels in Matthew (24:4-36) and Luke (17:23-24, 37; 21:8-36) also are recognized as apocalyptic in language and outlook. For example, Mark 13 depends heavily on the apocalyptic vision of the coming of the Son of Adam, found in Daniel 7. In Mark's hands, that vision becomes a source of inspiration for the expectation that the risen Jesus will return in victory to triumph over the forces of wickedness and usher in the full realization of the kingdom of God.

Second, some of the difficulties in this chapter stem from the fact that Mark has grouped some sayings that deal with contemporary historical events with others that appear to be about the future coming of the Son of Adam. A third group of sayings deals with the need for vigilance but without an explicit reference to either historical events or the apocalyptic vision of the End. Most scholars view the sayings in verses 1-8 as references to the destruction of the Temple in A.D. 70 by the Romans. Others, wanting to retain the traditional idea that Mark's community and Mark's Gospel originated in Rome, see these descriptions of historical catastrophes and severe trials as a reflection of the persecution unleashed against Christians in Rome by Nero.

However, since Mark sets the story in the context of a conversation between Jesus and his disciples about the Temple, the catastrophes described here are probably those that overtook Judea during the Jewish rebellion of A.D. 66–70. In Mark's story, Jesus predicts the Temple's destruction, which may indicate that Mark wrote his Gospel around that time. Undoubtedly, such a catastrophe would cause the early Christians in Mark's community to believe that the end of the world was upon them and the return of Christ near at hand. The question of Peter, James, John, and Andrew implies as much.

However, Jesus' reply is that the Temple's destruction, along with wars, natural disasters, and false messiahs, signals not the end itself but the beginning of the end. The signs mentioned correspond to the onset of a pregnant woman's labor. They are signs of the end in a similar way that labor is the sign of the end of pregnancy. The labor must be endured before the end can come; nevertheless, the end is assured. An expectant mother knows that the end of pregnancy is a birth. So these signs, while pointing to the end of the old order and the present age, also herald the dawn of a new age for the world.

Living into the Text

It is natural for us to want to know whether our trials and struggles have a deeper meaning. Do they point to something? This is especially true in times of war or when natural disasters strike or when we suffer grievous personal losses. Like Peter, James, John, and Andrew, we may feel like it's the end of the world. Think about some time in your life when you felt that it was "the end of the world." How did you deal with those feelings? Did you allow them to make you bitter and resentful? Did you give up hope? Or did you, like Jesus' disciples, try to find some greater meaning or catch a glimpse of the "big picture"? Did you discover the seeds of a new beginning in that experience, or were you trapped in feelings of despair?

Through Jesus' dialogue with his disciples, Mark warns his community against falling prey to false hopes and false messiahs as it struggles in a painful present to catch a glimpse of a better future. "Beware that no one leads you astray." During a time of great stress or trial, we all face the danger of looking for quick fixes and easy solutions. Con artists abound, religious ones no less than psychological and material ones. Someone is always around to try to tell us why we're experiencing the difficulties we're in, what the significance of our pain and struggle is, and how we can get out of it. The price exacted by these con artists is high, however. Disillusionment, a sense of betrayal, and the loss of our freedom to choose can all be more deadly than the struggle itself. When were you tempted to look for easy answers to your time of trial?

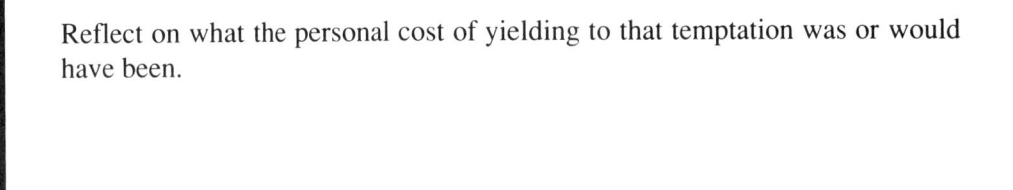

Reflect on what the personal cost of yielding to that temptation was or would have been.

Continue to reflect on the end-of-the-world feelings you've had. Can you see how that situation or those feelings might be (or might have been) different if you view (viewed) them as "the beginning of the birthpangs" rather than as the end in an absolute and tragic sense? What in you or your situation is (was) struggling to be born?

Close your time of reflection by giving thanks for the new birth(s) God has produced, or is producing, in you.

Living out of the Text

In the world around you, what causes you the most anxiety, causes you to ask when the end is coming? Is it famine in Africa, civil war in European nations, or the drug culture in the cities of the United States? Try to imagine what in those situations could be a sign, not only of the end, but also of a new beginning. How can your presence and attention (or that of your church) shorten the labor process? What good news can you proclaim?

DAY 4

ENDURING TO THE END

Preparation

As you settle in to your time of prayer and reflection on scripture, use the following Advent Antiphon to prepare yourself mentally:

*O Root of Jesse, who stands for an ensign of the people,
before whom kings shall keep silence
and to whom the Gentiles shall make their supplication:
Come, and deliver us, and tarry not.*

You may also wish to hum or sing the stanza of "O Come, O Come Emmanuel" derived from this antiphon:

*O come, thou Root of Jesse's tree,
an ensign of thy people be;
Before thee rulers silent fall;
all peoples on thy mercy call.
Rejoice! Rejoice! Emmanuel shall
come to thee, O Israel.*

Scripture: Read Mark 13:9-13.

These verses, like those in verses 1-8, appear to refer to actual or predicted historical events that Mark's community, as well as Jesus' disciples, could expect to face. The references to being "beaten in synagogues" and the betrayals within families may well reflect the situation in which members of Mark's community found themselves. The internal dissension that arose in Jewish synagogues between those who accepted Jesus as the messiah and those who did not, led to increasingly sharp disputes. These disputes ultimately resulted in the Christians' separation from the main body of Judaism late in the first century. Families often were divided. In any family feud, emotional intensity is high, so it is understandable that such painful divisions should raise questions about faithfulness and endurance. Nevertheless, this time of suffering and painful separation is a time for mission. It is a time to "stand before governors and kings because of me, as a testimony to them."

Living into the Text

At what time in your life have you felt that your loyalty to your personal beliefs and values caused the serious misunderstanding or conflict with family members, friends, or colleagues? How did you deal with the conflict? Did you compromise your convictions? Did you adopt the pose of the suffering martyr? Did you endure silently but without wavering in your loyalties? Did you retaliate in anger? If you have never experienced conflict as a result of your faith, you might want to explore why you have not. Is your faith too harmless to threaten your relationships? Do your relationships include persons whose commitments to Christ are weaker than yours? Do you think they must be right, and therefore you must be wrong?

Even if you have not experienced personally the sharp and angry conflict about which Jesus warned his disciples, try to think of a situation in your life or relationships where loyalty to Jesus could be costly; where you might be misunderstood or rejected by others close to you. To explore this issue another way, ask yourself if anything about your relationship to Christ would offend those who do not wish to be as committed.

As you think of ways in which your faithfulness has been, or might be, perceived as a threat by others who disagree, imagine what enduring "to the end" might mean for you. Is such endurance passive or active? How is Jesus' exhortation about enduring to the end related to his statement that "the good news must first be proclaimed to all nations"? What is the relationship between endurance and proclamation?

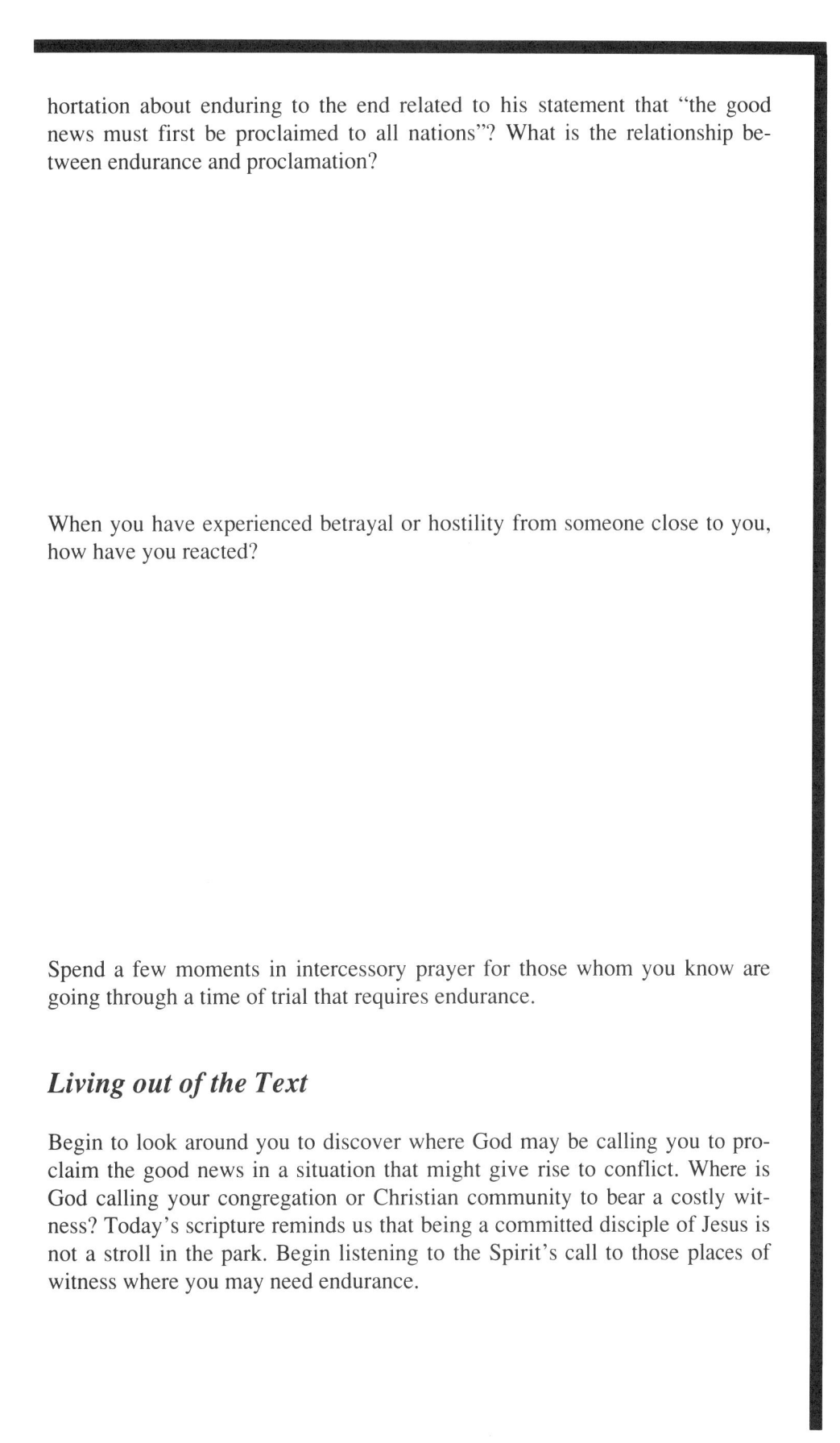

When you have experienced betrayal or hostility from someone close to you, how have you reacted?

Spend a few moments in intercessory prayer for those whom you know are going through a time of trial that requires endurance.

Living out of the Text

Begin to look around you to discover where God may be calling you to proclaim the good news in a situation that might give rise to conflict. Where is God calling your congregation or Christian community to bear a costly witness? Today's scripture reminds us that being a committed disciple of Jesus is not a stroll in the park. Begin listening to the Spirit's call to those places of witness where you may need endurance.

DAY 5

DISCERNING THE TRUE END

Preparation

Spend a few moments centering your mind and spirit. Breathe deeply, relax your muscles, and use a prayer phrase repeated in the rhythm of your breathing. ("My God and my all" was a favorite centering prayer of Saint Francis of Assisi.) Steadily gazing at a visual aid (icon, cross, or candle) can help you focus on God. Just saying the name Jesus while slowly inhaling and exhaling is a time-honored way of centering. Pray the fifth Advent Antiphon:

> *O Key of David and Scepter of the house of Israel,*
> *who opens and no one shuts, who shuts and no one opens:*
> *Come, and bring forth from prison the captive*
> *who sits in darkness and in the shadow of death.*

You may also wish to sing or hum the stanza of "O Come, O Come Emmanuel" derived from this antiphon:

> *O come, thou Key of David, come,*
> *and open wide our heavenly home.*
> *The captives from their prison free,*
> *and conquer death's deep misery.*
> *Rejoice! Rejoice! Emmanuel shall*
> *come to thee, O Israel.*

Scripture: Read Mark 13:14-23.

These verses also appear to relate to contemporary or expected historical events rather than to the final coming of the Son of Adam, since they include instructions to flee to the mountains. This and other references would make little sense if the ultimate end were in view. Probably the severe sufferings mentioned here are those that accompanied Jerusalem's destruction by the Roman armies.

The phrase "the desolating sacrilege set up where it ought not to be" is a direct allusion to the same phrase in Daniel 9:27; 11:31; and 12:11. The verses in Daniel referred to the act of the Syrian tyrant Antiochus IV, who offered a pagan sacrifice in the Temple. Mark offers that sacrilege as an analogy to help his community understand the similar defilement of the Temple by the Romans. The Temple's defilement did not lead to the end of the world in the time of Antiochus. And this defilement does not mean that the ultimate end is just around the corner, though the severity of the sufferings will cause many to think as much.

The sufferings predicted here are penultimate in nature; they point to the end but are not the immediate precursors. The warnings about false messiahs suggest that the attitude necessary to deal with these sufferings is a discerning vigilance. Such discernment will enable the elect to be faithful in a time of great trial.

Living into the Text

One of the temptations that arises when we face a time of severe testing or suffering is the temptation to turn it into a catastrophe; that is, to look at our troubles as the worst situation imaginable. The problem with this temptation is that no one can really deal with a catastrophe. By seeing our situation as catastrophic, we make it difficult—if not impossible—to find a way out or to summon up the courage to endure in hope. Instead, we often begin grasping at straws (false messiahs) in desperation; or worse, give in to despair. What we need is the ability to discern the true significance and gravity of our situation so we can act appropriately.

Think of the worst problems you face right now or ones you have faced recently. How have you been tempted to turn them into catastrophes? Which "false messiahs"—quick-fix solutions or solutions that promise deliverance *from* your dilemma rather than deliverance *in* your dilemma—have tempted you? Bring that painful situation or seemingly insoluble problem before God. Pray for discernment so that you can see it in its true light. You may wish to write in your journal about it. Often the act of writing about our problems brings clarity and helps us gain perspective.

Since discernment has a corporate dimension, you may find it helpful to discuss your situation with your pastor, a trusted friend, or someone else skilled in spiritual guidance. Persons who are not emotionally involved in our problems are not as prone to see them as the "end of the world."

Churches, as well as individuals, have a tendency to turn problems into catastrophes. Frequently, this tendency centers around financial problems and anxieties about meeting the budget or around declining attendance or membership. False messiahs often take the form of programs or gimmicks for attracting more people or raising funds. Sometimes restructuring can be a false messiah.

Even more frequently, our tendency to see catastrophes grows out of an unwillingness to face painful situations truthfully. Rather than being faced openly and honestly, strained relationships with another church member or with the pastor are often camouflaged behind denial, projection of our feelings onto someone else, displaced anger, or blaming. This internal dishonesty skews our perception of the situation, and molehills become mountains. The frantic search for false messiahs may reflect our own egocentrism and emotional dishonesty. How does your congregation or faith community face such a time of testing with its temptation to turn problems into catastrophes? How are you seeking discernment, or are you seeking discernment at all? How can you enable your church or community to begin that process of seeking discernment?

Close your time of reflection and meditation with the Lord's Prayer. "Give us this day our daily bread" is a petition, which if prayed honestly, offers an alternative to turning problems into catastrophes.

Living out of the Text

Our world faces many seemingly unsolvable problems. Some of them appear, and indeed are, catastrophic in scope and intensity. Identify a particular social issue or human problem that touches you or your faith community that seems hopeless to you. Begin to pray, by yourself and with others, for discernment so that you can see that issue in its true light. As the Spirit gives you discernment, be alert to the possibilities for faithful witness within the context of that issue or situation.

DAY 6

THE SIGNS OF THE END

Preparation

Center yourself using the Jesus Prayer ("Lord Jesus Christ, Son of God, have mercy on me ") or another short prayer phrase that you repeat slowly and rhythmically. Then pray the sixth Advent Antiphon:

*O Dayspring, Brightness of the light eternal
and Sun of justice:
Come, and enlighten those who sit in darkness
and in the shadow of death.*

Again you may wish to sing or hum the related stanza of "O Come, O Come Emmanuel."

*O come, thou Dayspring, come and cheer
our spirits by thy justice here;
disperse the gloomy clouds of night,
and death's dark shadows put to flight.
Rejoice! Rejoice! Emmanuel shall
come to thee, O Israel.*

Scripture: Read Mark 13:24-31.

In these verses, the scene shifts from historical catastrophes that point toward the end but are not the end themselves, to the true End, the coming of the Son of Adam in power and glory. The language here is reminiscent of the language of Daniel 7, particularly verse 26. Now the imagery is not historical but cosmological: the signs of the advent are a darkened sun and moon, falling stars, and the shaking of the heavenly powers. This passage, and others in the New Testament that use similar language, suggests that the earliest Christian communities had to rethink their expectations about the messiah's coming and the end of the age. Jesus' crucifixion forced such a change. Those faith communities that identified Jesus as the messiah had to explain why the messiah, rather than immediately establishing the kingdom of God in its full glory, suffered defeat at the hands of his enemies and was killed.

    Jesus' resurrection gave the early Christians the clue they needed to revise their understanding of history. Since many Jews already believed in the resurrection of the dead at the end of the age, the earliest Christians, who were

Jews, interpreted the resurrection of Jesus within that framework; it was an end-of-the-world kind of event.

Jesus' resurrection was not merely a spiritual experience or the resuscitation of a corpse but a new and powerful creative act of God. Just as God called Adam into life from the dust, so now God had called his faithful messiah to life from the dust.

This new act of creation was the *beginning* of the end of the world. Jesus' resurrection was the certain sign that the messiah would come again in glory to consummate the rule of God over all creation. The church now existed in an interim time—between the beginning of the end and the culmination of the end. Within the New Testament, this new understanding of history was expressed most clearly by Paul, whose writings are among the earliest Christian documents we possess.

Mark shares this perspective. Mark's concern is that interim time in which the church now exists. He is trying to help the members of his community see that the severe sufferings they are being called upon to endure do not signal the immediate and glorious return of Christ. Their sufferings are occasions for faithful imitation of Christ's sufferings and for engaging in mission to proclaim the good news. Yet those sufferings do point to the true end that will certainly come for those who trust in God's power as Jesus did. In other words, for those who follow Christ in faithful witness and endurance, the end will mean for them what it meant for Jesus—life from death and not destruction. Such is the nature of Christian hope.

Living into the Text

Several different ways of understanding human history are current in our world. Some views of history are cyclical: Everything that happens has happened before and will happen again. Religions such as Buddhism and Hinduism are grounded in such views of history and human existence. For those who hold to such views, salvation consists in somehow getting off this endless wheel of existence, either by achieving Nirvana (a sort of blissful nothingness, though bliss must be interpreted here as cessation of suffering and illusion) or by becoming One with the World-soul (according to Hinduism; some New Age thinking shares similar views).

Another way that we in the modern world understand history is the materialistic view, where history itself takes the place of God and moves according to natural, social, and economic forces. Marxism represents this view.

A third perspective is that human history has no meaning apart from the meaning that individuals give it. Individualistic, Western cultures often share this personalistic view.

The historical understanding that dominates the Bible is that history has both a beginning and an end. God's creative acts began the historical process, and God actively participates in the historical process to bring it to its intended goal. God allows human beings to act in freedom, thereby contributing to history's direction. Human actions, particularly those that arise out of human arrogance, greed for power, or selfishness, may hinder but cannot ultimately thwart God's creative and guiding will. God works in, with, through, and sometimes despite the actions of human beings to bring about the final realization of the creative purpose. Such an understanding gives us a framework for interpreting the meaning of Jesus and our own personal place and participation in history.

Which understanding of history—the cyclical, the materialistic, the personalistic, or the biblical—provides the framework for your own decisions and actions? How does your understanding of history affect your decisions and behavior?

In what way does the idea of Jesus' resurrection from the dead as the beginning of the end make sense to you? Does the biblical view that history ultimately will come to God's desired end make you uncomfortable, or does it reassure you? Though Mark's language about Christ's return is highly metaphorical, he is speaking about a real coming. If Mark is right in affirming that we live in the interim between the beginning of the end and the culmination of the end, what meaning does that give to your life? to the church?

Jesus was faithful to God, even through his sufferings, because he trusted in God's creative power to call forth life from death. He experienced the power that enabled him to bear faithful witness. Mark suggests that the members of his community will also experience God's power in their own time of trial. God will enable them to serve as faithful witnesses also. In what experiences have you felt that God's power was the only thing standing between you and failure or disaster? How did that experience make you feel? exhilarated? frightened? hopeful? confident? embarrassed?

If God is moving history toward its appointed end, what implications does this movement have for the way you currently live? What impact does it have on your priorities? your relationships? How does it influence your behavior? Does your behavior really matter?

Does it imply that all Christians have a vocation, a calling from God; and if so, how are we to live out that vocation? What would have to change in your life if you began to take the truth of Christ's return seriously? Be as specific as you can.

We pray "Your kingdom come. Your will be done, on earth as it is in heaven." Close your time today by praying that single petition, repeating it several times. Try to imagine the earth if God's will is truly done—particularly in you! Imagine what your life would look like if you anticipate the ultimate realization of God's reign in your relationships, your priorities, and your behavior.

Living out of the Text

Do you see any signs in your own life, in the life of your faith community, or in the world around you that history is moving toward an End that is life and not death? What signs would be as dramatic and unmistakable as a darkened sun or falling stars? Could you or your church be a sign of Christ's coming?

DAY 7

WATCHING FOR THE END

Preparation

Spend a few moments in attentive silence. Listen to the quiet. If inner noise prevents you from listening, use a prayer phrase repeated several times to center yourself. After you have waited in a listening silence for several minutes, pray the final Advent Antiphon.

> *O King of the Gentiles and their Desired One,*
> *Cornerstone that makes both one:*
> *Come, and deliver us whom you formed*
> *out of the dust of the earth.*

If you've been singing or humming the stanzas of "O Come, O Come Emmanuel," sing or hum the last one today.

> *O come, Desire of nations bind*
> *all peoples in one heart and mind.*
> *From dust thou brought us forth to life;*
> *deliver us from earthly strife.*
> *Rejoice! Rejoice! Emmanuel shall*
> *come to thee, O Israel.*

Scripture: Read Mark 13:32-37.

The sayings in verses 28-31, apart from the context in which Mark has placed them, could refer to any events. In context, however, they connect with the sayings about the coming of the Son of Adam to gather the elect at the end of the age. The sayings in verses 32-37 reinforce the connection with the Son of Adam's coming. Jesus warns the disciples not to speculate about the timing of "that day." This echoes the warnings in the earlier part of the chapter against identifying present personal sufferings or social and political woes as signs of the imminent end.

The "day" will come when God, and God alone, decides it will. Darkened sun, falling stars, and cosmic upheaval will herald "that day" just as the budding and flowering of a fig tree in spring heralds the approach of summer. The stark contrast between the images of cosmic upheaval and the pastoral tranquillity of a budding fig tree jolts our imaginations. The first is a sign no one expects or wants to see; the second one, a sign that everyone expects to see and takes pleasure in seeing. The first is a sign that would be the occasion of stark terror, so unusual would it be; the second would only be unusual if it did not occur.

What are we to make of these diametrically opposite images? We are to conclude, as Mark strongly exhorts us, that only an unceasing vigilance will have us ready to welcome the arrival of the master of the house. "What I say to you, I say to all: Keep awake!"

Living into the Text

One of our great sins is that most of us do not pay attention. We simply go about our daily routines. The very fact that our days are routine is evidence of our lack of attentiveness. God often seems remote, but how could it be otherwise? God is undoubtedly present to us, but we are present to God only in fits and starts. Whole days may pass without any attempt on our part to look for the signs of the coming of the "Desire of nations" or of the presence of God in the ordinary stuff of our lives.

Where in the events and relationships that make up your life are you most aware of God's presence? Where do you feel God is absent? How do you experience that presence or absence?

If we cannot see the budding of a tree in the spring as a sign, is it likely we will be attuned to the darkening of the sun or the shaking of the powers of heaven? Does attentiveness to the one make comprehension of the other possible? What signs of Christ's coming are you able to identify? Reflect first on your own life. What in your life speaks of your hope and anticipation of the end of the age? Reflect on the life of your faith community. Where do you see signs of expectation and hope? Focus your vision farther afield; what in the world around you may point to the coming in power and glory of the Son of Adam?

What would it mean for you to "keep awake"? Be as specific as you can.

Close your time of reflection by spending some moments in intercessory prayer for those whose needs are known to you and are within your area of concern.

Living out of the Text

Begin to look around you for a situation or an issue where you have been inattentive and where your attention and vigilance is needed. What or who could benefit from your willingness to speak or act as the Holy Spirit leads you? If you are part of a reflection or study group, consider this as a group project.

WEEK ONE

Group Meeting

Gathering

Depending on the makeup and preferences of the group members, you may use a variety of formats for the gathering time. The purpose of this time is to enable the members of the group to bond with one another so as to make the discussion and sharing more productive and open. Use one of the following suggestions or devise your own way of opening the group session.

* Sing several choruses of praise to God. An accompanist—either guitar or piano—will help greatly.
* Ask a group member (chosen in advance) to lead in devotions.
* Ask the group members to share a period of attentive silence together, perhaps about five minutes. Concentrate on becoming open to one another and open to the Spirit who is present.
* Lead a period of directed prayer. Guide the prayer time by mentioning specific petitions or needs of which you are aware and then allow a moment or two of silence for the group members to pray for that need.

Sharing the Journey

1. Ask members to share an initial reaction to the week's exercises. If the group is small (five to seven persons), each person may share. If the group is larger (up to twelve), allow four or five persons to share. This time is not for detailed discussion, just general impressions. Was the material on Mark 13 useful, difficult, strange, or eye-opening?

2. Give some attention to Mark 13's portrayal and understanding of history and human existence.[1] Consider the following questions:

How does Mark's picture of history's moving toward an ultimate end with the return of Christ in glory strike modern people?

Is such a worldview archaic or relevant?

How does the writer's description of Christ's resurrection as the beginning of the end and of the present in which the church lives as an interim between the beginning of the end and the culmination of the end, help our understanding of Mark 13?

Focus primarily on personal reactions and perspectives: What does it mean to me to say in the words of the Apostles' Creed, I believe that "[Jesus] will come again to judge the living and the dead"?

3. Ask members to share which of the week's exercises had the most telling impact on their lives and why. Not everyone may be comfortable in sharing this information. Encourage as much personal sharing as possible. When we are willing to be open to one another, we discover the meaning of Christian community.

4. Discuss the perspective on present sufferings or trials that Mark 13 offers. Consider the matter of signs:

What is a sign?

What does it signify?

How are we to interpret present sufferings as signs? What are the implications for one's (or one's faith community's) spiritual journey?

Closing

Spend some moments in attentive silence. Then join hands and sing the first stanza of "O Come, O Come Emmanuel."

---

[1] For more information on the biblical view of history and Christ's resurrection as the "beginning of the end of the world," see articles on "Eschatology," "Parousia," or "Second Coming" in *The Harper's Bible Dictionary* or *The Interpreter's Dictionary of the Bible*.

WEEK TWO

THE ANOINTED ONE

The annual church Christmas pageant, which is the Christmas story that most of us carry around in our heads, combines the traditions about Jesus' origins that we find in the Gospels of Matthew and Luke. We usually begin with the annunciation (Luke) and end with the visit of the Magi (Matthew), adding everything else in between. We often omit Matthew's slaughter of the innocents, because it's a real "downer," and we don't like to think about it at Christmas time.

This conglomerate Christmas story, however familiar we are with its outline and however sentimentally attached to it we may be, is a story of our own creation. Even a casual reading of the traditions in Matthew and Luke lets us see that the stories differ in both detail and purpose. The genealogies of Jesus in Matthew 1 and Luke 3, for example, have little in common. Nor do the two writers give the same date for Jesus' birth. Matthew dates the birth during the reign of Herod the Great who died in 4 B.C. Luke, on the other hand, dates Jesus' birth during the governorship of Quirinius who became governor of Syria in A.D. 6.

How are we to understand these differences? First, both Matthew and Luke wrote many years after the events they narrate, and both had to depend heavily on oral tradition for their information. They may have been the first ones to write down any of these orally circulated stories of Jesus' birth. Dating of events in the ancient world was not as precise as it is in the modern world, so the earliest Christian communities may have circulated several different traditions about the date of Jesus' birth.

Second, neither Matthew nor Luke's concern is to give an objective, newspaper-like account of the birth and life of Jesus. Both authors tell the story of Jesus with a specific purpose and a specific audience in mind, and their differing purposes and audiences lead them to select different stories from the oral tradition. In a very real sense, both Matthew and Luke were doing what we do when we tell our conglomerate version of the Christmas story; they were being creative writers.

In this study, we will spend a week on each set of traditions about Jesus' origins. We deliberately will not combine them as we usually do, so that we can discover something of the purpose and richness in each writer's telling of the stories.

We see Matthew's identity as a Jewish Christian leader writing to a predominantly Jewish audience from the very outset of his Gospel. The title, or superscription, in verse 1 tells us what Matthew thinks about Jesus—he is the messiah of Jewish expectation and hope. The word *messiah* means "anointed one." The messiah is God's anointed deliverer of God's people. The connection of the messiah with David was a prominent strand in Jewish messianic thinking. Under King David's rule, Israel reached its high-water mark in political, cultural, and economic terms. So persons naturally thought of the future hope of restoration and glory as a return to the glories of David's time.

However we do not find the title "Son of David" applied to the messiah in any of the Jewish messianic literature before Matthew. We do find this title in literature written about David's biological son Solomon. The traditions in this literature ascribed great healing powers to Solomon. Since Matthew also emphasizes Jesus as a healer, he may use the title "Son of David" in a dual sense: he is linking Jesus both to the healing tradition associated with Solomon and to the messianic expectation.

Matthew's genealogy further emphasizes the peculiarly Jewish cast of this Gospel. He traces Jesus' ancestry to David, and before David to Abraham, the patriarch of Israel. Luke, on the other hand, wants to establish Jesus' identity as the Savior of the world rather than as the messiah of Israel, so he traces Jesus' ancestry back to Adam, the universal human ancestor. Yet Matthew does not limit Jesus' significance to Israel. The salvation of the Gentile world is in view throughout the Gospel, present as a theme even in Matthew's genealogy and stories about Jesus' birth. His Gospel ends with the Great Commission, which is a mandate to "make disciples of all nations."

We will encounter other characteristics of Matthew's Gospel in the stories of Jesus' origins. One is his creative use of the Hebrew scriptures (Old Testament) to show that Jesus is the fulfillment of the hopes articulated by the Jewish prophets. Matthew also employs a sophisticated use of allusion to events and places in Israel's history that evoke memories and suggest meanings for interpreting Jesus' significance. For the original audience of Matthew's Gospel, the geographical place names have strong emotional and historical ties, ties rooted deep in memory. When Matthew's original readers read these narratives, they affirmed these places as "places in the heart."

DAY 8

THE MESSIAH'S FAMILY TREE
THE ANCESTRY OF HOPE

Preparation

As you settle into your place of prayer, take a few moments and center yourself, perhaps using a prayer phrase such as "O God, come to my assistance; O Lord, make haste to help me." Repeat the first phrase as you inhale and the second as you exhale. The object of repeating such phrases is to help you eliminate distracting thoughts and the call of daily duties and to focus your attention on God's presence with you and within you.

Meditate for a few moments on this ancient prayer of Origen, the great Alexandrian theologian of the third century:

> *Let us pray, however, the mercy of the omnipotent God to make us "not only hearers of" his "word," but also "doers" and to bring upon our souls also a flood of his water and destroy in us what he knows should be destroyed and quicken what he knows should be quickened, through Christ our Lord and through his Holy Spirit. To him be glory for ever and ever. Amen.*

Scripture: Read Matthew 1:1-17.

Matthew apparently made use of the genealogies in 1 Chronicles 2 and 3 to construct his own genealogy. Comparing Matthew's genealogy with the Chronicler's genealogies shows that he has not followed his source slavishly. Rather, he has arranged his material so that it fits into three sequences of fourteen generations each, following the customary practice of counting the last generation in each sequence as the first generation in the next.

Why fourteen? Possibly because the numerical equivalents of the Hebrew letters in the name "David" add up to fourteen or because fourteen represents twice seven, the number of perfection. At any rate, Matthew's audience would have appreciated the neatness of his scheme.

Of greater significance is what Matthew does with the genealogy. By tracing Jesus' ancestry to David and further back to Abraham the patriarch, he has rooted the birth of this baby squarely in the sacred history of God's saving acts. Having established Jesus' pedigree as "Son of David," he then proceeds to give that pedigree a shocking twist. Not only does he, against custom, include the names of women in his genealogy, but the women he includes—

Tamar, Rahab, Ruth, and Bathsheba—have two things in common. First, they are all women of questionable moral character in that all were, or could have been, accused of adultery. Mary shares this trait with them. So Matthew says something about God's ability and willingness to use surprising people in the history of salvation.

Second and more important, all (with the exception of Mary) were considered aliens or Gentiles. Tamar, Rahab, and Ruth were Gentiles by birth; Bathsheba was considered a Gentile because she married Uriah the Hittite. This latter fact probably explains why Matthew doesn't name her but refers to her as "the wife of Uriah the Hittite." By including Gentiles in the family tree of the messiah, Matthew gives us a clue to part of his agenda: the Anointed One is not the promised deliverer of the Jews only, but of all people.

By sharing in Jesus' ancestry, the Gentiles claim a place among the people of God. By Matthew's time, rabbinic commentaries already presented these women as heroic figures. Matthew is keeping with tradition in honoring them, but his use of them in a genealogy is unique.

Living into the Text

Many people take pride in their family tree, especially if they can trace their ancestry far back into the past. The taller the tree, the bluer the blood supposedly. However, most of us would like to prune some branches of our family tree. Certain ancestors' reputations damage our pride. Yet the family tree includes everyone—saints and rascals alike—and somehow, the line survived and events transpired so that we now exist to add yet another branch, making our own contribution to the future.

What is true for all of us was also true for Jesus. Not all the branches on his family tree were saints. His branches included good kings, wicked kings, a temple builder, a fratricidal murderer, and several persons of questionable morals. Yet out of that unlikely mix, came the One anointed by God to fulfill the hopes and dreams of all people.

Hope does not depend on ideal circumstances or perfect people. Hope is the result of God's working in the lives of generations of saints and sinners, heroines and rascals, to bring about the salvation of the world.

Spend a few moments reflecting on what you know about your ancestors. Where do you see signs of God's activity, perhaps despite the character or achievements of your ancestors? Reflect also on the fact that you, in some sense, are your family's hope for the future. What meaning does that fact have for you? Does it fill you with awe? dread? wonder? anticipation?

Matthew's inclusion of Gentiles, or aliens, in Jesus' family tree suggests that God does not share our distinctions between insiders and outsiders, us and them. What personal meaning does this suggestion of inclusion have for you? Who have you excluded from your life because of distinctions you have made or boundaries you have drawn? Ask the same question about your church: Who are the Gentiles, or aliens, who are outside the boundaries of "us"? What boundaries do you need to redefine?

Close your time by thanking God for the surprising grace that creates hope out of the most unlikely circumstances and uses the most unlikely people. Offer yourself as an agent of hope for the future of your family and your community.

Living out of the Text

Make an effort to think consciously about ways in which you could become a surprising agent of hope. After identifying your own "outsiders," begin to look for specific ways to eliminate those distinctions. Develop an action plan to change attitudes or behavior in order to make your life more inclusive.

Join your community's worship today. Ask God to allow you to offer genuine praise and to hear a clear word that will open up new insights or truths to you.

DAY 9

THE MESSIAH'S CONCEPTION AND BIRTH: GOD WITH US

Preparation

After a few moments spent in a centering silence, look again at the prayer of Origen in the exercise for DAY 8 (page 47). Meditate on his petition that God will "destroy in us what he knows should be destroyed." What in yourself needs to be destroyed? It may be certain addictive or compulsive behaviors; it may be a habit of mind that keeps you from growing and maturing; it may be harbored resentments or nursed grudges; it may be a habitual pattern of relating to others that injures or destroys intimacy and trust. Are you willing that these things be destroyed? Pray for discernment in identifying those things that need to be destroyed.

Scripture: Read Matthew 1:18-25.

In Matthew's story, Joseph is the principal character rather than Mary. An angelic messenger appears in a dream and announces the miraculous nature of Mary's conception to Joseph. The virginal conception and birth of Jesus does not appear to have played a significant role in the early church's thinking about Jesus. (It appears only here and in Luke's birth narrative.) Neither John nor Paul seem to have known this tradition. If they did know it, they did not think it important enough to mention. Nor does it serve as proof of Jesus' divinity either for the New Testament writers or the early church leaders. (See for example, Romans 1:3-4.)

It seems likely that at the time Matthew and Luke were writing, opponents may have brought charges that Jesus was an illegitimate child. The story offers a defense against such attacks by affirming that Jesus' conception and birth were a creative act of God, no less than was the creation of Adam and Eve. The repeated mention of the Holy Spirit's role links this story to the creation story in Genesis, where the spirit of God is the life breathed into Adam.

The idea of a virgin conception and birth would not have appeared strange to Matthew's contemporaries. Many heroic or prominent figures were portrayed as having been born of a union between a god and a mortal woman who was a virgin. Matthew's story is even more restrained than other stories. God is affirmed simply as the one who brings Jesus into existence by a new act of creation, and Mary is the instrument through whom this creative act is made manifest. The citation of Isaiah 7:14, with its mention of the name "Emmanuel," affirms Matthew's understanding of the significance of God's creative act. The young woman's giving birth to the child is a sign that God has not forgotten God's covenant promises or the sufferings of the covenant people.

Living into the Text

Matthew's story tells of Jesus' birth with quiet drama and dignity. Because he has traced Jesus' ancestry through Joseph back to David, Joseph is the principal character in the story. It is he who must face the scandal of his betrothed's pregnancy. It is he who receives the divine message about the true origins of this child, and it is he who must decide what to do in light of that message. By referring to Joseph as the "son of David" (the only time anyone other than Jesus is so described), Matthew may be linking Joseph with the Solomonic healing tradition also. By Joseph's willingness to accept Mary's baby as his own, he, in a sense, "heals" Mary by making it possible for her to remain within the community rather than becoming an outcast and possibly even being stoned to death as an adulteress.

Put yourself in Joseph's shoes for a moment. Try to imagine his reaction when he discovered that Mary was pregnant. Consider what a charge of adultery against Mary might have meant, both to her and to Joseph. What was the personal cost of Joseph's compliance with the heavenly messenger's instructions?

It often seems that following God's will demands the willingness to pay a price, sometimes a heavy price. What instances from your own experience can you remember in which you were conscious of a choice between alternatives, one of which was very costly? If you cannot remember having faced such a dilemma, can you imagine what in your current situation might present you with such a costly choice?

What does the name Emmanuel—"God is with us"—mean to you personally? Have you experienced Jesus as God with us in any concrete way you can describe? Where is God for you right now?

The name Jesus means "The Lord is salvation"; hence the angel's message, "For he will save his people from their sins." How do the two names, Jesus and Emmanuel, relate to each other? Address this question from the perspective of your experience. What does the notion of being saved from sin have to do with the notion of God's being with us? What does this tell us about the way God relates to us?

Close your time by meditating for a few moments on the phrase "God is with us." Let the phrase roll around in your mind.

Living out of the Text

"God is with us" is not only a personal and individual reality; Jesus' birth was a public birth, and the object of God's creative act was a people who needed salvation from their sins. As you go to work, spend time with your family, read the newspaper, and hear the news on television, choose some arena of human life or some issue facing your community and ask "What does it mean to say that God is with us? Where are the signs of God's presence?"

DAY 10

BETHLEHEM
PROMISES FULFILLED

Preparation

Meditate for a few moments on the following prayer by Origen.

> *Jesus, my feet are dirty. Come and slave for me; pour your water into your basin and come and wash my feet. I am overbold, I know, in asking this, but I dread what you threatened when you said: "If I do not wash your feet, it means you have no companionship with me." Wash my feet, then, because I do want to have companionship with you. And yet, why am I saying: "Wash my feet"? It was all very well for Peter to say that, for in his case all that needed washing was his feet: he was clean through and through. My position is quite different: you may wash me now, but I shall still need that other washing you were thinking of, Lord, when you said: "There is a baptism I must needs be baptized with."*

What are the "dirty feet" in your life that Jesus needs to wash?

Scripture: Read Matthew 2:1-12.

In this passage, Matthew has several themes going at once. He draws some parallels between the story of Moses' birth and preservation and the birth and preservation of Jesus the Messiah. King Herod becomes the new Pharaoh. The visit of the Magi appears to have its ancient parallel in the story told by the Jewish historian Josephus of a visit to Pharaoh by Persian astrologers who predicted the birth of a deliverer of Israel shortly before Moses' appearance.

Another theme connects with the tradition of Jesus' birth in Bethlehem. Unlike Luke, Matthew knows nothing of a journey to Bethlehem in connection with a census. His dating of Jesus' birth during the reign of Herod the Great would preclude such a journey, since the census mentioned by Luke didn't take place until about A.D. 7. Matthew's concern is not principally geographical. It is not Bethlehem as a place on the map that is important but Bethlehem as a place in the heart and in the covenant promises of God.

Prior to Matthew, persons already had begun to interpret Micah 5:1-2 messianically in some quarters of Judaism. Bethlehem, the city of David, is the birthplace of "the Son of David," the messiah. A paraphrase of the Hebrew text of Micah led to the wording "by no means least," whereas in Micah, the wording is "the least of the clans of Judah" (Micah 5:2, Jerusalem Bible). Bethlehem, a small and unimportant village in and of itself, nevertheless becomes the place where God fulfills God's promises of a deliverer.

Living into the Text

All of us have some sacred "places in the heart," places that have come to have special meaning for us because we associate them with important moments or important relationships in our lives. Many of us may have a Bethlehem, a place that speaks to us of God's faithfulness in keeping promises. It may be a particular church pew in which you have sat for many years and where you've had some wonderful experiences of God's presence and faithfulness. Your Bethlehem may be a town or a house in which you once lived (or are still living), where you became aware of God's presence in some special way. Going to that place, or returning to it after many years, immediately reminds us of promises fulfilled, of faithfulness experienced. Where is your Bethlehem? What memories or feelings does your Bethlehem evoke in you?

Bethlehem, in Matthew's spiritual geography, was not only a place of birth, nurture, love, and the homage of foreign magi; it was also the place of danger and risk. Herod knew the old prophecies as well, and his eye turned toward Bethlehem. Herod, like Pharaoh before him, represents the threat to God's promise of deliverance. If Herod has his way, God's promises will come to naught. Where in your own Bethlehem do you sense that danger was, or is, present? How are God's promises to you at risk because of that danger?

Bethlehem was an insignificant little place. It was certainly not a great city like Jerusalem and had little to recommend it. Yet David the great king had his roots there, and now Bethlehem becomes the birthplace of the "Son of David." Who would have expected anything extraordinary from such a place? God transforms insignificance into profound importance. In your Bethlehem, where do you see that transformation from "the least" to "by no means least" taking place? How do you see God's hand in that transformation?

Living out of the Text

Many people live in Bethlehem but have no idea of its true significance. For them it holds no memories of God's faithfulness, no sense that here in this little, out-of-the-way place a key moment or event in their lives is occurring. Look around you. Can you identify inhabitants of Bethlehem who don't have any sense of where they are? Do you know persons for whom Bethlehem has never become a place in the heart? How can you help them realize what really is happening? How can you bear witness to God's faithfulness?

DAY 11

EGYPT
REFUGE AND SLAVERY

Preparation

After a few moments of centering yourself in silence, pray again the prayer of Origen from DAY 10 (page 53). Origen, one of the greatest theologians of the early church, was a strong proponent of the allegorical method of interpreting scripture. Each detail in the text had a deeper or spiritual meaning underlying the plain or surface meaning. Obviously, Origen understands "dirty feet" in the metaphorical sense of "sins." First he prays for that washing from his sins. But he also prays for a deeper washing that Jesus' statement defines and symbolizes for him: "There is a baptism I must needs be baptized with." Meditate for a few moments on what Origen may have meant by this "other washing," and what such an idea might mean in your own life.

Scripture: Read Matthew 2:13-15.

Still drawing parallels between Moses and Jesus, Pharaoh and Herod, Matthew tells of Joseph's dream, in which an angel warns him of Herod's murderous plots against the Messiah. The mention of Egypt as a place of refuge could not help but evoke memories of the stories of the patriarch Jacob who, with his sons, fled the famine in Canaan and went to Egypt for refuge. God's providential care had sent Joseph into Egypt earlier, and God had aided Joseph in becoming the vice-regent of Pharaoh. Through Joseph, God preserved the patriarchs. God kept the promise to Abraham of many descendants.

Yet, while Egypt was a place of refuge where Israel flourished and grew into a multitude, it also became the place of slavery when "a new king arose over Egypt, who did not know Joseph" (Exodus 1:8). This new Pharaoh laid a heavy yoke of bondage on these foreigners who were flourishing to a dangerous extent in his land.

Matthew sees the flight to Egypt as the immediate solution to the threat to the Messiah's life. Yet if this solution is not temporary, it could result in a repeat of Israel's experience. While God's plan sends the holy family to Egypt, God does not will that the family stay there. "Out of Egypt I have called my son." Egypt is still a spiritual "place in the heart" for both Jews and Christians, retaining this dual character of both refuge and prison, preservation and slavery.

Living into the Text

We have all experienced something that had a promising beginning, which turned sour later. What began as a solution to a problem became an even worse problem. Think about a time in your life when you pursued a course of action that offered itself as a solution to a particularly pressing dilemma or problem. But, like Israel in Egypt, you stayed too long; the solution became a yoke of bondage. Where is your Egypt?

What in your life makes you feel trapped or enslaved? Did it begin that way? What changed in you or in "Egypt" to turn it from a refuge into a prison? What possibilities of deliverance or hope of freedom might the Anointed One offer you?

After reflecting on the meaning of "Egypt" for your own personal life, think about your church or faith community. Where do you see this same solution-turned-problem pattern at work in your life together? What began as a means of preservation but turned into an institutional "albatross" around your collective neck? To discover where "Egypt" is for your church, ask this question:

Where do you feel imprisoned by something that, at one time, may have had a positive character?

Close this time of reflection by thanking God for preserving you to this day. Ask God to help you discover where you have settled down and become so comfortable in "Egypt" that you are no longer free to follow the Spirit's leading.

Living out of the Text

Look at the situation in the community where you live or work. Where do you see people living in "Egypt"? What issues or situations have this double-edged character of refuge and slavery? What would it take to free those trapped in lifestyles or systems that have become oppressive? Begin to focus on an issue(s) that has the characteristics of "Egypt." Follow it until you discover whether and how you could bring hope of deliverance as a disciple of the Messiah.

DAY 12

RAMAH
PLACES IN THE HEART

Preparation

Sit comfortably and deliberately relax. Concentrate on one area of your body at a time, and consciously allow your muscles to relax. Breathe deeply and rhythmically, letting each breath draw you inward to God's presence. After a few minutes of this breathing prayer, focus on this ancient prayer of Saint Gregory of Armenia:

> *Mingle, O Lord,*
> *our humanity with thy divinity,*
> *thy greatness with our humility,*
> *and our humility with thy greatness,*
> *through Jesus Christ our Lord. Amen.*

Pray this prayer slowly and repeatedly until it begins to become your own.

Scripture: Read Matthew 2:16-18.

Traditionally, many Jews associated Ramah (a town about five miles north of Jerusalem) with Rachel, the wife of Jacob and the "mother" of Israel. According to tradition, Jacob buried Rachel in Ramah. Ramah also served as the staging place for the Exile when the armies of King Nebuchadnezzar II[1] of Babylon conquered Jerusalem in 586 B.C. and carried the leading citizens of Judea into captivity.

Among the captives was the prophet Jeremiah who had attempted unsuccessfully to prevent the war between Babylon and Judea. At Ramah Jeremiah was given the choice of accompanying the exiles to Babylon or remaining behind in Judea with the poor peasantry. He chose to stay with the peasants in the war-ravaged city as a sign of hope to the victims of the conquest that God would bring the exiles back.

When the exiles returned seventy years later, Ramah was the site of the first settlements. In Matthew's hands, Jeremiah's lament compares the Pharaoh's slaughter of the innocents to King Herod's actions. Again innocent children are killed; again Rachel weeps for her children. For Matthew, a new exile is underway. This time, the Messiah himself is being forced out of the land.

Living into the Text

Matthew's first readers, steeped in their religious history, could hardly remain unmoved by the powerfully evocative story of Herod's massacre of the children and the citation of Jeremiah's lament at Ramah that accompanies it. Coming immediately after his reminder of the Exodus, it leads his readers to feel that the the holy family's flight to Egypt is a new Exile and that the Lord's people are again the victim of a tyrant's brutality. Yet, despite Herod's raging and the grim memories of the conquest and exile, the reminder of Ramah also strikes a note of hope. Ramah was the symbol of exile, but it was also the place of return from exile. At Ramah, Jeremiah, by choosing to stay with the poor of the land, proclaimed God's faithfulness to his people and God's promises of a future restoration.

Reflect a few moments on the contrast between the themes and the moods evoked by this passage and the way our culture, even the church, often insists on focusing only on the happiness and joy of the Christmas story. When did you last hear (or preach) a sermon in which Herod's massacre was given its due weight as a major theme in the Nativity celebration? What does this say about our tendency to ignore or repress what is painful and ugly, even when it enters our own experience?

Where is Ramah in your personal life experience? Where is the place of your worst defeat? your greatest loss? Where have you felt exiled from your family, your closest friend, or even yourself? When have you felt like Rachel who could not be consoled because her loss was so great? What have you done with those feelings? ignored them? tried to forget them? become depressed by them? faced them head-on? Spend a few moments identifying your own Ramah. You may want to use the space below to write about your own experience of loss and exile.

Reflect on the fact that Mary, Joseph, and the baby Jesus, the Anointed One, went into exile in Egypt. Were they also exiled from God? If Jesus is Emmanuel—God is with us—what does this suggest about our own experiences of exile and loss? Where was God, or is God, in your own Ramah experience?

Remember that God didn't forsake God's broken people—not in Babylon, not in Ramah, not in ruined Jerusalem. Jeremiah, the "weeping prophet," was a living sign of God's continuing faithfulness and hope for the future. You may want to record your experience of hope in the midst of loss or your prayer for such hope in your journal or in the space below.

In your closing prayer, offer your own Ramah experience(s) to God, and ask the Lord to reveal the signs of Emmanuel's presence that will give you hope. If renewed hope is yours already, thank God for the means by which it entered your experience.

Living out of the Text

What situations or issues in your community or local area are characteristc of Ramah? For whose children is Rachel still weeping? How can you be a Jeremiah—a sign of hope—to those persons or in that situation? Think about this from a corporate point of view: Where is Ramah for your church or faith community?

---

[1] You will find the spelling variant "Nebuchadrezzar" in Jeremiah 25:1 and following. This variation is based on the Babylonian roots of the name. However, it is the same person who reigned as king in Babylon from 605–562 B.C.

DAY 13

NAZARETH
EXODUS AND DETOUR

Preparation

Use this ancient prayer of Margaret of Antioch to prepare yourself for your time of reading and meditating on the scriptures:

> *O Lord God, Ruler of the heaven and of the earth, Creator of things visible and invisible, Giver of eternal life, and Consoler of the sorrowful, make me to stand firm in the confession of thy name that as with thine aid I have begun the good fight, so with thine aid I may be deemed worthy to gain the victory, lest the adversary spitefully mock at me, saying: "Where is now her God in whom she trusted?"*
>
> *But let the angel of thy light come and restore to me the light which the darkness of my cell has taken from me; and let the right hand of thy majesty scatter the phantom hosts of the ancient enemy. For we know, O Lord, that thy mercy will aid us in all temptations.*

Meditate on the names Margaret used to address God. Notice how they move from the transcendent to the immanent, or from the cosmic and far to the personal and near. How does your own image of and relationship to God encompass both those dimensions?

Scripture: Read Matthew 2:19-23.

The parallels with Israel's Exodus story continue. If the holy family stays in Egypt, the place of refuge will become a place of slavery just as it did for Israel. Herod's (Pharaoh's) death signals that it is time to leave Egypt and head for Canaan, the land of Israel. In mentioning "the land of Israel" twice, Matthew calls attention to the motif of "the promised land," which played such a large part in Jewish religious life. However, just as the people of Israel who left Egypt under Moses' leadership had to make a forty-year detour in the wilderness, so the Messiah cannot return immediately to "the land of Israel," identified in this case as Judea with its cities of David—Bethlehem and Jerusalem.

Instead the Messiah goes to Galilee, a fact of great importance to Matthew. (See Matthew 4:15-16, where he uses the quotation from Isaiah 9:1-2 to affirm the Messiah's intention of including Gentiles in the kingdom of heaven.) For Matthew, Galilee has some parallels with the wilderness in the Exodus story. In Galilee, Jesus prepares for his ministry, experiences both success and frustration, learns dependence upon God and confidence in his vocation. The time in Galilee prepares him for the final stage of his journey—his entry into Jerusalem and the road to Calvary.

The early church was familiar with the tradition that Jesus' family settled in Nazareth, but Matthew gives special significance to this fact by serving it up as the fulfillment of prophetic expectation. He does not draw his quotation, "He will be called a Nazorean," from any known biblical text. Either Matthew is quoting a biblical text from an earlier and different edition than any we know or from a text later excluded from the canon. Perhaps he is playing off the Hebrew word for "branch" (Isaiah 11:1) for its similarity in sound to the word for Nazareth.

Living into the Text

Most of us remember a time in our lives when we thought we were on our way to the promised land, only to discover that we had to make a detour. Sometimes the detour seemed endless, and we thought we would never arrive at our goal. Perhaps some of us are still on the detour.

Imagine Joseph's feelings when he got the news that it was time to pack up and move, only to discover upon arrival, that the goal of his journey was not a safe place for himself and his family. What experience in your life corresponds to the experience of the holy family—heading for the promised land but forced to take a detour? How did (do) you feel about it? How did you deal (are you dealing) with those feelings and frustrations?

Often we are more aware of God's presence when our lives seem to be on track. Being aware of God's presence when we're forced into a detour is more difficult. Is it because we confuse God's presence with our convenience and desires? Or is it because the detour often involves hardship, and we're so preoccupied with meeting the hardship that we fail to see God's hand leading us?

Matthew reminds his own community of their spiritual history in the Exodus and thereby helps them understand the meaning of Jesus, as well as helping them see God in their own situation. While on the detour, Israel met

God at Mount Sinai and received the Law. In "Galilee of the Gentiles" (Matthew 4:15), Jesus discovered his own identity and vocation, called his core group of disciples, and enjoyed the favor of the crowds as they experienced the blessings of God's kingdom through his ministry.

When you have identified your detour, try to see where God is working to prepare you for your arrival in your homeland. As you answer the question, "Where is God in this detour?" you will hold the key to discovering its meaning for you. You may wish to record your reflections in your journal or in the space below.

Close your time of reflection by praying the Lord's Prayer.

Living out of the Text

Who among your family and friends is experiencing the frustrations of a detour? Pray for them, and pray to discover how you might be a sign of God's presence for them.

DAY 14

THE MOUNTAIN COMMISSION AND PROMISE

Preparation

Again today, pray the prayer of Margaret of Antioch from DAY 13 (page 62). Reflect on its appropriateness as a prayer for people on a detour. Notice her appeal for strength to stand firm in a time of severe testing and darkness.

In the prayer, she refers to "the light which the darkness of my cell has taken from me." As you look inward in silence, identify your own darkness and let Margaret's prayer become yours.

Scripture: Read Matthew 28:16-20.

By the end of the Gospel, when we stand on the mountain with the risen Jesus and his disciples, we know that this was where Matthew was leading us all along. We may have gone the long way round, enduring the frustrations of the detour, but our goal was to stand on the mountain with the risen Lord and hear him say, "All authority in heaven and on earth has been given to me. Go therefore and make disciples of all nations.... And remember, I am with you always, to the end of the age." All the "places in the heart"—Bethlehem, Egypt, Ramah, Nazareth—were stations on the way to this mountaintop. And this final place is not the end of the journey either. It is really only a jumping-off point, the end of the beginning.

Just as a graduation ceremony marks both the end of one stage and the commencement of a new stage, so does this passage. The end that has been reached is the end of the Messiah's historical ministry to the "lost sheep of the house of Israel" (Matthew 10:6), but it is the beginning of the Messiah's ministry to "all nations" through the mission of his followers. We ground our commission to go and make disciples in the ultimate authority granted the Messiah and which, by extension, is granted also to those who go in his name. A promise accompanies the commission: the Messiah, no longer confined by time and space, will be with those who are sent, even to the end of the age.

Living into the Text

The church often uses this text to motivate Christians to proclaim the good news of Jesus Christ to all the world. Often church members have narrowed the focus to the sending of missionaries to other lands and cultures, rather than accepting it as a mandate for every follower of Jesus. "All nations" is not a measure of geographical or cultural distance that defines a missionary or a mission field. A mission field is anywhere there are people who are not becoming disciples of the Messiah, and a missionary is anyone who is a disciple of the Messiah. Being a disciple of the Messiah means recognizing and living under the Messiah's authority in community with others who place themselves under the Messiah's authority.

In what ways are you consciously committing yourself to live under Jesus' authority and carry out his commission? How is that discipleship (discipline) visible in your lifestyle; in your relationships; in your decisions about your job, your money, your time, your pleasures, and your treatment of others? Discipleship is not an internal, spiritual, and private matter; it is a public confession and a public vocation. If you cannot describe how you are living out that discipleship, spend some time reflecting on your priorities, commitments, and use of resources. Pinpoint specific measures you will take to make that discipleship visible.

What would have to change in your life in order for you to become a disciple of Jesus? What would have to go? What would stay? What could stay only if you offer it to Christ for transformation by God's grace?

If you answer, "Yes, I am committed to being a disciple," or "Yes, I want to become a disciple," then begin to identify your mission field and the manner of your obedience to Jesus' commission. Where and how will you "go . . . and make disciples"? This process may involve naming your fears, as well as acknowledging your reluctance to carry out this commission.

Close your time again today by praying the Lord's Prayer. Think about each petition as you pray it. It is a prayer for disciples.

Living out of the Text

As you go about your work today or reflect on your day, begin to formulate some specific ways you can obey Jesus' commission to "go . . . and make disciples." This exercise goes beyond good intentions to the development of a disciplined action plan. To whom will you go? How will you go? Will you share the good news of Christ with someone you know? Will you involve yourself in the social or political arena to work for justice? Identify your mission field, and then go.

WEEK TWO

Group Meeting

Gathering

Follow the suggestions for gathering given for WEEK ONE (page 42), or devise your own. Allow some time for the group members to reestablish connections with one another and then, as a group, come to a point of focus.

Sharing the Journey

1. Take a few minutes for some generalized sharing of reactions to the exercises for WEEK TWO. Share initial impressions, surprises, problems with the format or content, difficulties experienced in getting into a regular and methodical approach to prayer and reflection on scripture.

2. Discuss reactions to the exercise for DAY 8. What reactions do you have to the exposition of Matthew's genealogy? to the tracing of one's own spiritual ancestry? to the suggestion that we may need to rethink our distinctions between insiders and outsiders on the basis of what Matthew has done with Jesus' genealogy?

3. Focus on Matthew's designation of Jesus as Emmanuel—God is with us. Try to give specific meaning to that phrase by sharing how you have (or have not) experienced "God is with us."

4. Consider the writer's connection between Matthew's treatment of Jesus' conception and birth and the creation story in Genesis. Is this interpretation helpful? Why or why not?

5. Reflect and share the exercises on the "places in the heart" (DAYS 10–14) that were most meaningful to you personally, and why? What "places" in your own individual journey are sacred to you? Reflect on this same question in the context of your life together as a church or faith community.

6. Think about and share which of the "Living out of the Text" suggestions had the most meaning for you personally. Which

seemed especially relevant for your church or group? Which of the suggestions are appropriate for your group or congregation to address together?

Closing

Take a moment or two and encourage persons to share prayer concerns. Then sit or stand in a circle, spending several minutes in a shared silence. Then name each of the expressed concerns, allowing thirty seconds or so of silent prayer for each one. After naming all the needs, join hands and pray the Lord's Prayer together.

WEEK THREE

THE SAVIOR

Luke and Matthew are the only New Testament writers who show any interest in the traditions about Jesus' origins. Matthew may have included stories about Jesus' origins—particularly the story in Matthew 1:18-25—to counter charges by opponents of his community that Jesus was an illegitimate child. However, that motive does not play much of a role in Luke's stories about Jesus' origins.

Luke uses the stories of Jesus' birth and infancy to introduce many of the themes that will appear throughout the Gospel and Acts (Luke's sequel to the Gospel): The importance of the Temple and Jerusalem as symbols of spiritual legitimacy; Jesus' identity as universal Savior, Messiah, and Lord; the Christian community as the continuation of, and to some extent, the replacement of Israel as the people of God; and God's gracious favor shown to the poor and oppressed. Many scholars believe that the songs of Mary (*Magnificat*), Zechariah (*Benedictus*), the heavenly chorus (*Gloria in Excelsis*), and Simeon (*Nunc Dimittis*) were liturgical songs, or psalms, used in early Christian worship even before Luke included them in his Gospel.

All this points to the probability that Luke's Gospel originated in a setting outside the context of early Jewish Christianity. The cosmopolitan tone and sophisticated literary style that follows Greek narrative and rhetorical patterns suggest a writer who was a Gentile, writing to a community of predominantly Gentile Christians. Luke tempers somewhat the sharp and often hostile language against the Pharisees and scribes found in Mark and Matthew. This Gospel reflects a predominantly Gentile church that is defining itself over against Judaism—perhaps for the purpose of legitimizing the church in the eyes of the Roman imperial power.

In the following exercises, the birth and infancy stories will serve as guides and clues to the significance of the angel's announcement to the shepherds, "To you is born this day in the city of David a Savior, who is the Messiah, the Lord." The emphasis is on the personal experience of confessing Jesus as Savior, Messiah, and Lord. What hopes and expectations might we find fulfilled in this one who is the Savior, not only of Israel, but of the whole world?

DAY 15

GOD'S SURPRISE

Preparation

Settle in to your time and place of prayer. Remember that you are here to meet God. To prepare yourself for that meeting, pray the following prayer of Saint Gregory of Nazianzus, one of the early Eastern church leaders:

> *God from all time, you were manifested to us in the fullness of time, so that by becoming [human] you might make me God. Thus, when I call on you, come as blessed and propitious God. Come to me with helping hand, O my propitious God. Save me, overwhelmed as I am amid war, and wild beasts, and fire, and storm. I have nowhere to turn my gaze except to God alone.*
>
> *From these O Christ, deliver me. Spread your sheltering wings about me always. O King, drive hateful cares far from your servant. Let not my mind be harassed by grave anxieties, such as this world and the prince of this world devise for hapless mortals. They corrode the godlike image within as rust corrodes iron.*

Scripture: Read Luke 1:5-25.

Twenty-four divisions made up the Aaronic priesthood (see 1 Chronicles 24:1-19). Each division or class performed the priestly duty of offering the incense in the temple in Jerusalem one week during the year. Due to the number of priests in each division, the opportunity to perform this function possibly could come only once in a priest's lifetime. At this climactic moment in Zechariah's life, God intervenes in a surprising way.

As the text suggests, Zechariah did not expect such a concrete answer to his and Elizabeth's prayers. His fear at being confronted by an angel is consistent with the portrayal of other such confrontations in the scriptures. (See Judges 13 where Manoah, Samson's father, receives similar news; and Isaiah 6 where the prophet receives his call.) The angel decisively answers Zechariah's doubtful response, "I am an old man," with the words: "I am Gabriel. I stand in the presence of God." Zechariah's silence is both a judgment on his failure to believe God's promise and a gift that allows him time and space to prepare for God's wonderful surprise.

Certain elements of Judaism were looking for a messiah. Some began to expect the prophet Elijah's return in preparation for the messiah, because Elijah had not died but had been taken directly to heaven. Luke interprets John the Baptist's ministry in terms of that expectation. He appropriates Israel's sacred history for his own predominantly Gentile church.

Living into the Text

When have you hoped and prayed for something for so long that you gave up hope and more or less accepted that it would never happen—only to have it happen as a complete surprise? How did that surprise make you feel—awed that it happened at all? afraid? joyous? irritated that it took so long? all of these at once?

What situation in your life (or in the life of your congregation or faith community) is like Zechariah and Elizabeth's situation? For what have you been waiting and praying without results?

Zechariah and Elizabeth had resigned themselves to a life without children, which in their culture, was a life without God's blessing. Yet they continued to live faithfully. "Both of them were righteous before God, living blamelessly according to all the commandments and regulations of the Lord." Zechariah continued to perform the priestly office, despite his resignation. What might this suggest about the situations in which we have resigned ourselves to settling for less than what we'd hoped for? What connection, if any, do you see between the way Zechariah and Elizabeth lived and God's surprise?

The angel announced to Zechariah that he and Elizabeth would have "joy and gladness, and many will rejoice at his birth." Then why was Zechariah so afraid to believe the angel? How do you deal with God's surprises? An old proverb says, "Be careful what you pray for; God may answer your prayers." What is there about the possibility that God might answer your prayers or fulfill your deepest desires that makes you afraid? Where in your life do you voice Zechariah's plaintive, "But I am an old man"?

God's surprise for Zechariah and Elizabeth served a larger purpose than simply enabling them to be parents. Their child would "turn many . . . to the Lord their God." Sometimes when we receive God's surprises, we get caught up in our feelings of fear or gratitude or joy, and we fail to look for a larger purpose. We focus on our own needs or feelings, much as Elizabeth did. Her response was not one of thanksgiving related to God's preparing the way for the messiah. She was simply thankful that she would no longer suffer the social stigma of barrenness.

But then, Elizabeth didn't see and hear the angel. Without an angelic announcement, how can any of us look beyond our immediate reactions and feelings to grasp the larger picture? Where in your life do you feel the need to see some larger plan or purpose? How might your situation become the means of preparing the way for the Lord?

Close your time by thanking God for the surprises of grace and by asking for deeper insight into the larger picture.

Living out of the Text

Look beyond your own situation to the situation of your church, the community in which you live, or the larger public arena. Where do you see a hopeless situation, a situation where resignation has set in and expectation for the future has died? How might God's surprises break in and change the situation? Might you or your church be that surprise? How might such surprises prepare the way for the Lord?

Join in worship with the members of the body of Christ. To be authentic, you must root your prayers in the prayers of God's people.

DAY 16

GABRIEL'S NEWS

Preparation

Use the prayer of Gregory of Nazianzus from DAY 15 (page 72). Gregory's affirmation that "by becoming [human] you [God] might make me God," sounds strange to our ears. Yet this affirmation was, and still is, central to the understanding of salvation in the Eastern Orthodox tradition. By assuming our humanity, God makes it possible for us to assume our true identity as beings created in God's image, divinized humans as it were. During this time of preparation, repeat this phrase several times, using the form of Saint Athanasius: "God became human that I might become divine." Allow your mind and heart to absorb this ancient, yet ever-new truth.

Scripture: Read Luke 1:26-38.

The phrase "in the sixth month" effectively links this story with the story of the announcement of John's birth to Zechariah and Elizabeth. In the sixth month of Elizabeth's pregnancy, the angel Gabriel appears to an unexceptional young woman in a provincial town in Galilee. We do not know Mary's qualifications or why God chose her as the bearer of the messiah. The message is everything.

However, something of Mary's character comes through in her response to the message. When the angel tells her that she will conceive and bear a son whom she will name Jesus (see Matthew 1:20-25 where Joseph, the legal father, names Jesus), Mary's first response is supremely practical, "How?" Good question! The angel's reply is the key to Luke's understanding of this birth. In his Gospel, Luke often links "Spirit" and "power." Here the linkage (as in Matthew) recalls the Genesis creation story. The Spirit goes forth from God, acting as the agent of God's power to create life from chaos or primeval matter. Mary need not trouble herself with the "how." God's spirit will overshadow her, creating new life by the power of God. The child will be holy, meaning "set apart." This distinctiveness names him as "Son of God."

At this point Mary's character shines through, and she becomes a model for all would-be disciples. Faced with frightening and incomprehensible news she responds simply, "Here am I, the servant of the Lord; let it be with me according to your word."

Living into the Text

The angel's announcement to Mary came as a surprising grace. She "found favor with God," but we are not told why. God's evaluation of us rarely corresponds to our own standards of worthiness or unworthiness. God's grace came to Mary unexpectedly, with no reference to her state of readiness. When have you received, like Mary, an unexpected gift? Perhaps the gift (or grace) came through another person, perhaps through a set of circumstances. Were you aware of its nature as a gift, and did you connect that gift with God's grace?

Perhaps Mary wondered if this unanticipated gift would cost her more than it was worth. Being told that she would have the high privilege of becoming pregnant out of wedlock—with all the risk of a broken engagement and social ostracism or worse—we could understand if she had said, "Thanks, but I'll pass." Have you ever felt like that?—That perhaps God wanted too much of you; that God's grace, freely given, carried too high a price tag? Think about the graces in your life from that perspective. Dietrich Bonhoeffer spoke of "costly grace," which is always free but never cheap. Where in your experience are you aware of such "costly grace"? In what areas is the price tag too high?

Consider Mary as a model of discipleship: "Here am I, the servant of the Lord; let it be with me according to your word." If we take them seriously, three of the most difficult words to say are, *Let it be*. They encompass a world of trust and risk, confidence and vulnerability. What situation in your personal life, your family life, or your church life has such a promising and frightening aspect? What will it cost you to say with Mary, "Let it be with me according to your word."

Close your reflection with a time of silence, meditating on Mary's example. When you feel ready and have mustered all the faith, courage, and commitment you can, pray that risky prayer, "Here am I, the servant of the Lord; let it be with me according to your word."

Living out of the Text

Begin looking today for that point of vulnerability and trust that requires concrete action. Start to form an action plan. To whom do you need to speak? What do you need to do? Where do you need to go? Where do you need to let go? How will you do it? What resources are available to you? Act!

DAY 17

ELIZABETH'S BLESSING

Preparation

Gregory of Nazianzus was one of the most poetic pray-ers in the early church. In the following prayer, allusions to the Exodus story, the Exile, and the destruction of Sodom and Gomorrah all mingle powerfully to carry his petitions.

Save me, save me, Immortal,
from the Enemy's hand;
let no evil-doing defeat me
or Pharao[h] torment me;
let me not be his captive,
Christ, your Opponent's;
let him not wound me and drag me
to hard-hearted Babylon.

I would live forever in your temple,
singing your praises,
safe from the showers of Sodom,
from the flames on the head,
all evil dispelled by the shadow
of your powerful hand.

Meditate on this prayer for a few moments. Where might "hard-hearted Babylon," a place of cruel captivity, be for you? Can you confidently trust in Christ's power to deliver you as Gregory did?

Scripture: Read Luke 1:39-45.

This story of Mary's visit to Elizabeth and Mary's song of praise (the *Magnificat*) that follows provide a link between two narrative passages. Although Luke mentioned earlier that Elizabeth was related to Mary (the only place that implies a blood relationship between John the Baptist and Jesus), he gives no reason for Mary's visit to Elizabeth. The visit seems to be the necessary narrative means of bringing Mary and Elizabeth together so Elizabeth can pronounce a blessing inspired by the Holy Spirit. It also brings John the Baptist and Jesus together in a prenatal encounter.

Elizabeth's characterization of Mary as "the mother of my Lord" points to two things. One is Luke's intention to establish the order of priority between John and Jesus. John may be born first, but he is born to prepare the way for the greater life to follow. A second point of interest is probably not Luke's intention. The story suggests that by the time Luke wrote his Gospel near the end of the first century, the church was beginning to venerate Mary already. Certainly the liturgical elements of the "Hail Mary" are here in Gabriel's and Elizabeth's greetings. And it is a short step from "mother of my Lord" to "mother of God," the title accorded to Mary in some church quarters from the second century onward.

Living into the Text

If we see Luke's portrayal of Mary as a model of faithful discipleship, perhaps his portrayal of Elizabeth models joyful humility. After waiting so long before conceiving and being the senior woman, it would have been understandable had she insisted on the importance and priority of her own child. Instead, she joyously pronounces Mary blessed because of the child she is carrying. Elizabeth pronounces herself blessed to be in Mary's presence because she herself dared to believe that God would fulfill the promise made to her and Zechariah.

Think of a person you know who exemplifies the kind of joyful humility modeled by Elizabeth. In what ways is such humility a sign of weakness? of strength? How does one come by it?

Where in your own life do you see the need for such a strong and joyous humility? Where do you see self-centeredness, self-interest, or self-will most prominently displayed?

Elizabeth's humility appears to be linked with patience and hope. She "believed that there would be a fulfillment." Her wait was a long one. Her circumstances were improbable at best and virtually nil at worst. Yet she waited, hoped, and trusted. And when the promise finally came, she believed that God would fulfill it.

Most of us are impatient people; our cultural training encourages us to expect instant gratification. What situation in your life causes you to be most impatient? Where do you most need to wait in hope and believe in God's faithfulness?

As far as you are able, let go of the situation that is making you feel impatient and anxious. Imagine yourself placing that situation or problem in God's hands and leaving it there. Then get up and go about your work or take your nightly rest, freed from your burden.

Living out of the Text

Look for a problematic situation in your community or workplace or church that needs patient hope rather than instant gratification—a place where you might become an Elizabeth who could be God's agent of blessing. Be specific in your analysis of the problem, so that you can be specific in seeing your role in bringing blessing.

DAY 18

MARY'S PRAISE

Preparation

Again today enjoy and ponder the poetic beauty of this prayer by Gregory of Nazianzus, letting its petitions become your own as you center yourself for your time with God:

I rise and pledge myself to God
to do no deed at all of dark.
This day shall be his sacrifice
and I, unmoved, my passions' lord.
I blush to be so old and foul
and yet to stand before his table.
You know what I would do, O Christ;
O then, to do it make me able.

Scripture: Read Luke 1:46-56.

Mary's song of praise, or the *Magnificat*, is an early Christian hymn or psalm of praise. Some early traditions and the early church writings originally attributed it to Elizabeth. However, Luke's community clearly attributes it to Mary, which reflects the growing importance of Mary in the Lukan church.

Its model is Hannah's song in 1 Samuel 2:1-10, and it is full of allusions to various phrases from the Old Testament. The emphasis is not on Mary herself but rather on God's mighty acts of salvation, of which Mary is the blessed recipient. These mighty acts have a universal scope and purpose; the promise made to Abraham and the ancestors of Israel are promises for "all generations." The emphasis on social reversal and God's raising up of the poor and lowly is a strong Lukan theme. (See the citation from Isaiah 61:1-2 as Jesus' description of his own vocation in Luke 4:18.) It gives concrete shape to the purpose and outcome of God's saving acts.

Living into the Text

The term *Savior* is an important one for Luke. Mary rejoices in "God my Savior." In chapter 2, the angel of the Lord will announce to the shepherds: "To you is born . . . a Savior." In the context of Mary's song of praise, what concrete meaning(s) does *Savior* have? Whom does God save? In what sense is God Mary's savior? How does God save? From what does God save? To what end does God save?

What specifically does the idea of God as a savior mean to you? From what in your life do you need saving? What would such salvation look like for you? What would change? How would it (you) change?

Clearly Luke understands the meaning of Savior, not only in an individual sense but in a social sense as well. Salvation, whatever it means on the personal level, also involves the casting down of the mighty and the exalting of the lowly, the feeding of the hungry and the sending of the rich away empty.

John Wesley, Methodism's founder, declared that he knew of no holiness that was not social holiness. How does this notion of salvation square with the individualistic idea of salvation that American Protestant churches often have preached and taught? How does Luke's idea of savior compare or contrast with the popular notion of "accepting Jesus as my personal savior"? What implications for your own life and for the life of your faith community do you see?

The *Magnificat*, while being a beautiful psalm that has inspired some of the greatest music and art down through the centuries, is a radically subversive statement. It gives no comfort to the rich and the powerful to be told that they will be dethroned and dispossessed and that this will be the saving work of God. How can someone who is rich or powerful hear this song as good news? How can you hear it as good news?

Close your time of reflection by praying or singing or listening to a recording of a musical rendition of the *Magnificat*. Let the cadences and images of this powerful and beautiful song penetrate your mind and heart. Join your praise with Mary's for God's salvation.

Living out of the Text

Look at your newspaper or watch the TV news today and analyze the main issues and events in terms of the understanding of salvation in the *Magnificat*. What would salvation look like if it came to the persons, communities, and situations described? Then begin to ask yourself how you and your church or faith community could become a witness to that salvation. Be as specific as you can.

DAY 19

ZECHARIAH'S PROPHECY

Preparation

Spend some moments in centering prayer, perhaps using a prayer phrase such as "My God and my all," repeated silently until your distractions have begun to fade into the background. Then ponder this prayer of confession by Gregory of Nazianzus. What truth about yourself do you see in it?

> *I have deceived myself, dear Christ, I confess it;*
> *I have fallen from the heights to the depths.*
> *O lift me up again, for well I know*
> *delusion came because I wanted it.*
> *If I presume again, I'll fall again,*
> *and fall to my undoing. Take me to you*
> *or I die. It cannot be that I*
> *alone shall find you hard and unresponsive.*

Scripture: Read Luke 1:57-80.

Comparing this story of John the Baptist's birth with the account of Jesus' birth and infancy in chapter 2 immediately makes the parallels between the two clear. For example, compare 1:57-58 with 2:6-7 and 1:59-63 with 2:21. The movement in both stories is birth, circumcision and naming, the work of the Holy Spirit, the praise of God in a hymn, and the child's growth in physical and spiritual strength. Luke adds other material as well, but he clearly intends the obvious parallels between the birth of John and the birth of Jesus.

We may explain these parallels in part as the technique of good oral and literary storytelling; they help the reader or hearer remember the stories. But Luke wants to link the significance of these two births as well. For Luke, the mission of John is not separate from that of Jesus. He does not, for example, report John's imprisonment nor suggest that Jesus' ministry began only after John's had come to an end as do Mark (1:14) and Matthew (4:12-17).

In Luke 7:18 and following, John's questions to Jesus, conveyed through John's disciples, are motivated by his confusion about the role of Jesus in God's saving history rather than by any doubt brought on by his own arrest and imprisonment, which are not mentioned. Luke understands God's work of salvation—from the creation of the world through the covenant with Abraham through the Gentile mission of the church—as one continuous whole. Luke traces Jesus' ancestry not only to Abraham but to Adam, the universal human ancestor. The "mighty savior," of whom Zechariah speaks in this ancient liturgical song, the *Benedictus*, arises out of Israel. The savior's mission is to "the ends of the earth" (Acts 1:8). John's role, then, is to prepare the way for the savior, but both his mission and the savior's mission are part of God's larger mission.

Living into the Text

As suddenly as Zechariah lost his ability to speak, he regains it after confirming in writing Elizabeth's announcement that their son will be named John. As soon as his speech returns, described here as something over which he had little or no control—"his mouth was opened and his tongue freed"—and his first words are praises to God. It is interesting to note the effect Zechariah's regaining of his speech has upon his neighbors. Luke tells us that "fear came over all their neighbors, and all these things were talked about throughout the entire hill country of Judea."

When have you ever experienced feelings of fear? When has your faith community evidenced such fear at the unexpected manifestation of God's presence or power? Sometimes this fear emerges at the mere thought or possibility of doing something that might bring us into an immediate experience of divine power.

If your pastor or a member of the church suggests holding a healing service, or a newcomer to the congregation testifies to having spoken in tongues, why is fear often a common response? Try as much as possible to personalize this question: What aspects of an unexplainable or unexpected manifestation of God's presence and power make you afraid? Why?

Zechariah's prophecy describes God's saving work in the covenant with Abraham as having a purpose: "That we . . . might serve him without fear, in holiness and righteousness." What is the relationship between salvation and deliverance from fear? What is the relationship between the absence of fear and the service of God in holiness (being set apart or called out) and righteousness (justice)? Again, personalize this question. From what fear do you need deliverance? How might such deliverance express itself so that your life would be recognizably distinct from the world around you by your concern for justice?

Verse 77 describes John's mission as giving the people the "knowledge of salvation," the result of "the forgiveness of their sins." John Wesley understood this connection. In describing his Aldersgate experience, he said, "I felt I did trust in Christ, Christ alone for salvation, and an assurance was given me that he had taken away *my* sins, even *mine*, and had saved *me* from the law of sin and death." The Methodist tradition often has called this knowledge of salvation "assurance" or the "witness of the Spirit." Wesley believed, not only that all people needed to be saved and could be saved, but that all could *know* that they were saved. He believed this inner assurance was the work of the Holy Spirit. (See Romans 8:14-17.)

Think of sins, not so much as wrong acts, but rather as attitudes, values, and behavior that result from failing to live in holiness; that is, as set apart from the attitudes, values, and behavior of the world. This failure to live a called-out life produces a corresponding failure to be righteous (just). What would "forgiveness of sins" mean in your case? In what areas of your life are you failing to live in holiness and righteousness? Where have you "bought into" the world's values, attitudes, and behavior? Where are you a captive to fear? How can a person live a holy life, a life that is distinct from the world's value systems, strictly as an individual? Is some form of disciplined community an essential part of holy living?

Close your time of reflection by confessing your own failure to live a holy life, and begin to ask God to give you that inner witness of the Spirit that Luke describes as "the knowledge of salvation." I say "begin to ask," because it seems that few of us become aware of our own lack of holiness all at once. It may take some time for us to become fully aware, both of the depths of our own sinfulness and the abundance of God's forgiving love.

Living out of the Text

Make some time to watch television today. Pay special attention to the attitudes, values, and behaviors that the programs and commercials promote. Which of them are consistent with what you are beginning to understand as "holiness and righteousness"? Which are incompatible? Which of them have already "hooked" you? It may be beneficial to make a list as you watch. Use it as a checklist as you continue to reflect on what holiness and righteousness mean in your own life.

DAY 20

THE PEOPLE'S JOY

Preparation

Begin your time today with Gregory of Nazianzus's prayer, in which he identifies with two thieves—Adam and the repentant thief crucified with Jesus. Let the power of Gregory's confession and plea carry you with him into that same identification.

> *Alas, dear Christ, the Dragon is here again.*
> *Alas, he is here: terror has seized me, and fear.*
> *Alas that I ate of the fruit of the tree of knowledge.*
> *Alas that his envy led me to envy too.*
> *I did not become like God; I was cast out of Paradise.*
> *Temper, sword, awhile, the heat of your flames*
> *and let me go again about the garden,*
> *entering with Christ, a thief from another tree.*

Scripture: Read Luke 2:1-21.

While it is not possible to reconcile Luke's dating of Jesus' birth with Matthew's (see the discussion on page 53), Luke tells us something extremely important. Luke's story emphasizes that the momentous act of God signified by this birth took place in the most mundane of circumstances—in a government census designed to collect taxes. Our imaginative retellings of the Christmas story dramatize the arrival at a crowded inn, a rude or sympathetic innkeeper, the scene at the stable. They have little in common with Luke's strangely terse account. In concise, almost spare, language he reintroduces Joseph and Mary, tells of Mary's delivery of a child, and explains her laying the child in a manger. No hoopla or drama—just the bare details.

Originally, it appears that the story of the angels and the shepherds was a separate tradition from 2:1-8. In the joining of the two traditions, we now find Luke's characterization of Jesus as "savior" combined with another christological title, "Christ the Lord." The *Gloria in Excelsis* that the angels sing, like the *Magnificat* and the *Benedictus* before it, appears to have been in liturgical use when Luke incorporated it into his story. Only the shepherds receive this celestial visit and hear of the significance of the birth. Even Mary and Joseph are amazed at the shepherds' news (2:16-19). Both the angels' song and the shepherds' praise emphasize that this birth is God's work.

Living into the Text

You may need to distance yourself from the Sunday school Christmas pageant version of the story of Jesus' birth to read and hear it afresh from Luke. How could such a momentous event take place, apparently unnoticed by anyone but a few shepherds? Even they knew of it only as the result of a visit by the heavenly host. What does this imply about the way God acts in this world? What does it suggest about the way we identify an event as God's action?

Where or when in your life has something happened that seemed mundane and insignificant at the time, but later you became aware that God was at work? How did that realization dawn on you?

The angel's announcement was that the birth of this child was "news of great joy for all the people." The angel connects this joy with the identity of this child as "Savior." And "Savior" somehow relates to the experience of God's peace. In the *Benedictus*, Zechariah sang that "the dawn from on high will break upon us . . . to guide our feet into the way of peace." Here the angels' song proclaims, "On earth peace among those whom [God] favors." How do you understand the relationship among *joy*, *savior*, and *peace*? How are they connected for you personally? If you do not connect them, what would have to happen in your life to make those connections?

Close your time by singing "Angels We Have Heard on High." Join the praise of the shepherds.

Living out of the Text

The shepherds, after visiting the child, began to tell others what they had seen and heard. Well, who wouldn't talk after an appearance of singing angels! The point is, however, that they didn't keep the news to themselves. In order for the news to become "great joy for all the people," all the people had to hear about it.

How are other people hearing about the news of great joy from you? If you are not sharing that news, why not? How have you experienced the news as great joy? From what have you been "saved"? Do you not share the news with others because you feel incompetent to do so? Spend a few moments thinking about specific ways you might share the news of a great joy. With whom are you in frequent contact? Explore your networks.

DAY 21

SIMEON'S INSIGHT, ANNA'S PRAISE

Preparation

Settle in to your place of prayer. Then end this week as you began it, using a prayer of Gregory of Nazianzus, which in many respects sums up the whole enterprise of spiritual growth.

*Labour awaits you, soul, great labour,
if you would know yourself,
the what, the whither, and the whence,
the way of now behaving—
whether it should be as it is
or whether more is expected;
labour awaits you, soul, and a purer life.*

*If you would ponder on God and probe
into his mysteries,
if you would know what was there before
the world and the world itself—
the source from which it came to you,
the end that will take it from you:
labour awaits you, soul, and a purer life.*

*If you would know how God guides the helm
of the world and the course he plots,
why he set some things like rocks in the sea
while others he left in flux—
why [humans] most of all are caught in the stream
and swirl of perpetual change:
labour awaits you, soul, and a purer life.*

*If you would show me my former glory,
the shame that has come to succeed it,
what binds me to this mortal life
and what my end will be—
if you would hold this light to my mind
and drive dark error from it:
labour awaits you, soul: may it not undo you.*

Scripture: Read Luke 2:22-38.

There is nothing comparable to this narrative in Matthew's birth and infancy stories. Nor does Luke's narrative contain a parallel about John the Baptist. The nearest scriptural allusion may be Hannah's dedication of Samuel to God in 1 Samuel 1. But even if Luke associated that event in his mind, he tells about the presentation of Jesus very differently. The main focus is on Simeon and the vision that he articulates in yet another ancient liturgical song that is still very much alive in current worship. The *Nunc Dimittis* (2:29-32), as it is commonly known from the Latin of its first line, is a psalm of praise to God for the fulfillment of hope in the divine promises.

The text describes Simeon as "righteous and devout, looking forward to the consolation of Israel, and the Holy Spirit rested on him." He is a man who lives toward the future rather than the past or present. And because God always is bringing the future into the present, Simeon's eyesight (or insight) is sharp enough to see the future that God is bringing in the person of this child. The hymn has a missionary thrust. God's salvation is "a light for revelation to the Gentiles and for glory to your people"—a motif that is also one of Luke's main concerns.

Though all the Gospel writers mention women in the company of Jesus, Luke particularly emphasizes the role of women in his Gospel. We have seen Zechariah and Elizabeth, Joseph and Mary; and now Luke links Simeon with Anna, an elderly prophetess. (See the list of women among Jesus' followers in 8:1-3.) By the time of Luke's writing, the status of women was well-established in the early church, a status that appears to have been accorded them by Jesus himself, as well as by their role as witnesses of the resurrection. Otherwise it is hard to explain the prominence of women in a narrative produced in such a highly patriarchal society. So Anna's praise, while not in the form of liturgical song, nevertheless is rooted in the same forward-living expectation and hope that characterized Simeon's.

Living into the Text

All of us tend to see what we're looking for. Something may be right in front of our eyes, but if we're not looking for it, we'll miss it. Many people (and many churches!) look toward the past. Someone has said that the seven last words of the church are *We've never done it that way before*. Others live totally oriented to the present. What's happening *now* is more important than either what happened in the past or what is expected or hoped for in the future. Both past and present are important, of course.

Simeon was rooted in traditions from the past. His devotion to the traditions of Israel led him to the Temple that day. The Spirit that guided him was the same Spirit that guided the great prophets. Nor was Simeon oblivious to the present. He had to live very much in the present to be sensitive to the voice of the Spirit. But his orientation was to the future. He was looking for something, for "the consolation of Israel." And so he saw God's future when he took a baby in his arms.

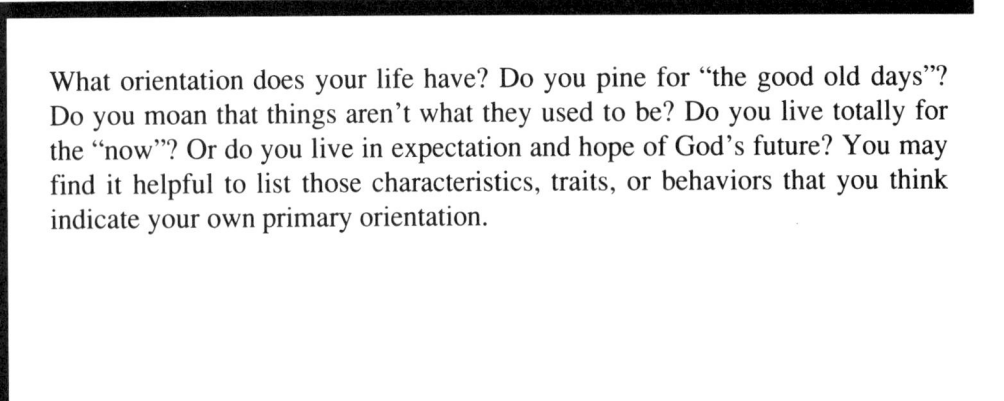

What orientation does your life have? Do you pine for "the good old days"? Do you moan that things aren't what they used to be? Do you live totally for the "now"? Or do you live in expectation and hope of God's future? You may find it helpful to list those characteristics, traits, or behaviors that you think indicate your own primary orientation.

For Simeon and for Anna, the definition of living a full and fulfilled life was the experience of seeing God's future in the Christ child. What is your definition of a full and fulfilled life? How does one recognize such a life? How does one's orientation toward the past or the present affect that recognition?

What, for you personally, would be the equivalent of "the consolation of Israel" or "the redemption of Jerusalem"? In other words, what would allow you to praise God with Simeon and Anna and say, "Now you are dismissing your servant in peace . . . for my eyes have seen your salvation"?

Luke specifically links Anna's insight to her constant prayer. What link can you affirm between a prayerful life and the ability to live in hope of God's future and to recognize that future as it comes toward us? Answer this personally: What is the link between *your* prayer life and your ability to live in hope?

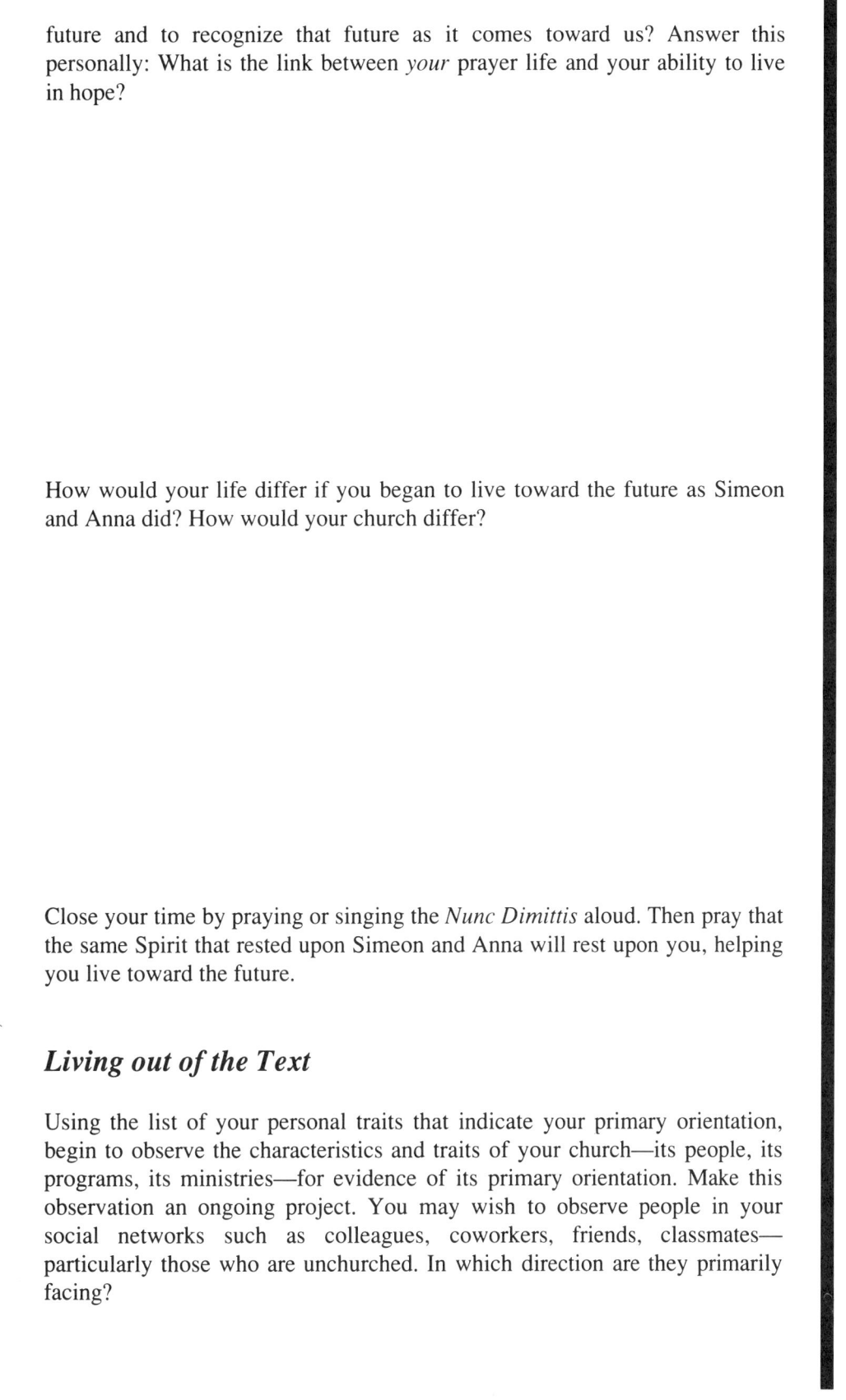

How would your life differ if you began to live toward the future as Simeon and Anna did? How would your church differ?

Close your time by praying or singing the *Nunc Dimittis* aloud. Then pray that the same Spirit that rested upon Simeon and Anna will rest upon you, helping you live toward the future.

Living out of the Text

Using the list of your personal traits that indicate your primary orientation, begin to observe the characteristics and traits of your church—its people, its programs, its ministries—for evidence of its primary orientation. Make this observation an ongoing project. You may wish to observe people in your social networks such as colleagues, coworkers, friends, classmates—particularly those who are unchurched. In which direction are they primarily facing?

WEEK THREE

Group Meeting

Gathering

Be sure that by now you know the names of everyone in the group. Begin your time together by reading aloud (or singing if you know a musical arrangement) the *Magnificat*. Let Mary's hymn set the mood of your meeting.

Sharing the Journey

1. Take a few moments for general sharing about the week's exercises.

   Which of the characters in Luke's narrative spoke most strongly to you?

   Which of the liturgical songs did you find most meaningful?

   In what ways were the scripture notes helpful or obtrusive?

   What were your reactions to the prayers of Gregory of Nazianzus?

   How helpful were the "Living out of the Text" suggestions?

2. Share, if you are willing, experiences of frustration or resignation at some long-delayed wish or dream. Use Zechariah's story in the Temple to spark your own memories of delayed dreams and frustrated longings.

3. Tune in to Mary's experience of grace—an unhoped for and unexpected gift. When have you felt similarly graced? How did you identify the event, situation, or experience as a gift of grace?

4. Ask the following questions:

   What was your attitude toward Mary before this week's exercises? What is it now?

> *Can Mary be rescued as a model of spirituality from the near-divinity she has been accorded or the obscurity in which she has been forgotten?*

Share your own difficulties in saying Mary's words "Let it be to me according to your word."

5. Pause in your discussion to read aloud or sing the *Benedictus.*

6. Explore with the group the connections you discovered among *joy*, *savior*, and *peace*. Share as personally as you feel comfortable with the others in the group. Our stories are more powerful than our ideas.

Closing

Pray or sing together the *Nunc Dimittis*. Spend a few moments in silent meditation. Then suggest that persons voice prayers for themselves or the church, asking for the ability to live toward the future as Simeon and Anna did.

WEEK FOUR

THE WORD

The Gospel of John has been an enigma since it first appeared on the scene.[1] Some early church interpreters referred to it as a "spiritual" Gospel to distinguish it from the Gospels known as Matthew, Mark, and Luke. Was that description a way of saying that John was harder to understand than the others or was it a way of saying that it was of more value to the church or contained a higher truth than the others? Certain Christian communities have preferred the Gospel of John to the other Gospels, beginning with some of the Gnostic Christian sects of the second and third centuries. Today, John is the preferred gospel in those churches labeled "evangelical," primarily for its spiritual quality. The Gospel of John often serves as the basis for evangelistic tracts, and John 3:16 is one of the few Bible verses that fans display on banners at football games.

It is easy to discover the reason for the enigmatic character of the Gospel of John. Even the casual reader immediately notices the difference between this Gospel and the other three we have in our Bible. Parts of John are like the other Gospels—narratives about things Jesus did, most of them miraculous. John tells the narratives in the third person just like the other three Gospels. Yet John's stories themselves are different. John tells of healings and miraculous feedings, but they are not the same healings or miraculous feedings narrated in the other Gospels.

However, what really strikes the reader as unique about this Gospel is the way the writer intersperses these third-person stories with long, rhetorical speeches of Jesus, which he delivers in either the first or second person. In these speeches, the earthy, concrete, everyday flavor of the stories disappears; a highly mystical, theological, grandiloquent, and timeless flavor takes its place.

In this Gospel, it is not easy to distinguish among the voices of the narrator, John the Baptist, or Jesus. All speak in the same high-blown fashion. An older generation of commentators preferred the mystical, timeless, and highly theological speeches of the Fourth Gospel to the Jesus who speaks in the Synoptic Gospels because they considered John's Jesus to be a universal figure purged of parochial Jewish elements.[2] Having read the Dead Sea Scrolls, we now know that such mystical, theological discourses were thoroughly Jewish.

In this final week of our spiritual exercises, we will concern ourselves with some of these discourses of the Jesus of the Fourth Gospel. "The Word" (*Logos*) is a controlling image in John's Gospel. Not only is Jesus himself understood as "the Word"; but if believed, the word of Jesus gives eternal life (5:24); the word abides in those who believe it (5:38); those who keep Jesus' word will not die (8:51); the word is from the Father who sent Jesus (14:24); Jesus' word cleanses his disciples (15:3); and their safety and unity in the world depends on the fact that Jesus has given them the word (17:8, 14). We will begin the week with this image and return to it on Christmas Day. Be sure to do the Christmas Day exercise on Christmas, regardless of the day of the week on which it falls. In between, we will examine some of the "I am" discourses of Jesus. We will focus on discovering who this Word is for us.

---

[1] In what follows, I am drawing, not only on my own study of the Fourth Gospel, but on the work of current scholars, principally Robert Fortna. The introduction to his book *The Fourth Gospel and Its Predecessor* (Philadelphia: Fortress Press, 1988) gives a lucid description of the perplexing character of this Gospel, which is accessible to the literate layperson as well as to the professional biblical scholar.

[2] As Fortna points out, this preference often was the result of a thinly veiled anti-Semitism.

DAY 22

THE WORD IN THE WORLD

Preparation

Use this prayer of Ambrose of Milan to begin your time of reflection today. Ambrose was the spiritual father of Saint Augustine, one of the greatest Latin theologians of the early church. As you pray this prayer, meditate on Ambrose's thought expressed so fervently: The purpose of our salvation is that we might enjoy God.

> *Lord, who hast mercy upon all, take away from me my sins, and mercifully kindle in me the fire of thy Holy Spirit. Take away from me the heart of stone, and give me a heart of flesh, a heart to love and adore thee, a heart to delight in thee, to follow and to enjoy thee, for Christ's sake. Amen.*

Scripture: Read John 1:1-13.

In this prologue to the Gospel, the prosaic intrusion of verses 6-8 interrupts the flow of the magnificent and poetic hymn to the *Logos,* or "Word," somewhat jarringly. Most likely, this bit of concrete information is the work of a redactor (editor) who wanted to make sure that the Gospel readers understood the relationship between John the Baptist and Jesus as a relationship between light and its reflector. If we leave out these two verses, what remains flows seamlessly through verse 18, though we will reserve verses 14-18 for our Christmas Day meditation.

For years, scholars have recognized the *Logos* hymn as a meditation on the meaning of Jesus, inspired by the creation story in Genesis. There God spoke, "Let there be light." And God's spoken word created light. God spoke; light was! In the theology of the Fourth Evangelist, God's word still brings forth light; God's word *is* light and life; and in the person of Jesus, that creative, light-producing, life-giving, eternal word is coming into the world of space and time—into the world of human history. From beyond time and history, the eternal, creating Word enters and becomes subject to history. "He came to what was his own, and his own people did not accept him." The Fourth Evangelist displays no interest in birth and infancy stories. Perhaps he did not have access to such stories; or as is more likely, he simply wished to base his interpretation of Jesus on the creation story of the divine *Logos.*

Living into the Text

The writer makes it clear that the Word brought life into existence, and we experience this life as a light shining in darkness. Whenever we turn on a light in a dark room or shine a flashlight outside on a dark night, we're immediately aware that light, in a sense, brings a world into being. We see what is there as we could not see it before turning on the light. We enter a dark room, and we see nothing. We flip a switch, and suddenly we see a sofa, a chair, a TV set, a picture on the wall, and a cobweb in the corner.

Imagine that your own inner life, your "heart," is a dark room. It is a world, but a world that is "a formless void" (Genesis 1:2). Now imagine that the eternal, creating Word enters that room. The Word doesn't have to turn on the light; the Word is the light. Suddenly the formless void dissolves into real shapes and forms. The light is shining in the darkness. What does it reveal? What do you see in your inner life? Spend some time looking and identifying what you see. What furnishings of your inner life are good and beautiful? What are the "cobwebs" in the corners?

"He was in the world, and the world came into being through him; yet the world did not know him. He came to what was his own, and his own people did not accept him." Theologically, John is saying, "This eternal, creating word of God has entered the risky, 'real world' human situation and has become vulnerable just like all the rest of us."

When have you experienced that sense of coming to what was your own and meeting with rejection or indifference? How did you feel? angry? betrayed? hurt? lonely? How many of those feelings have you found in the dark places of your inner life since the light has illuminated them?

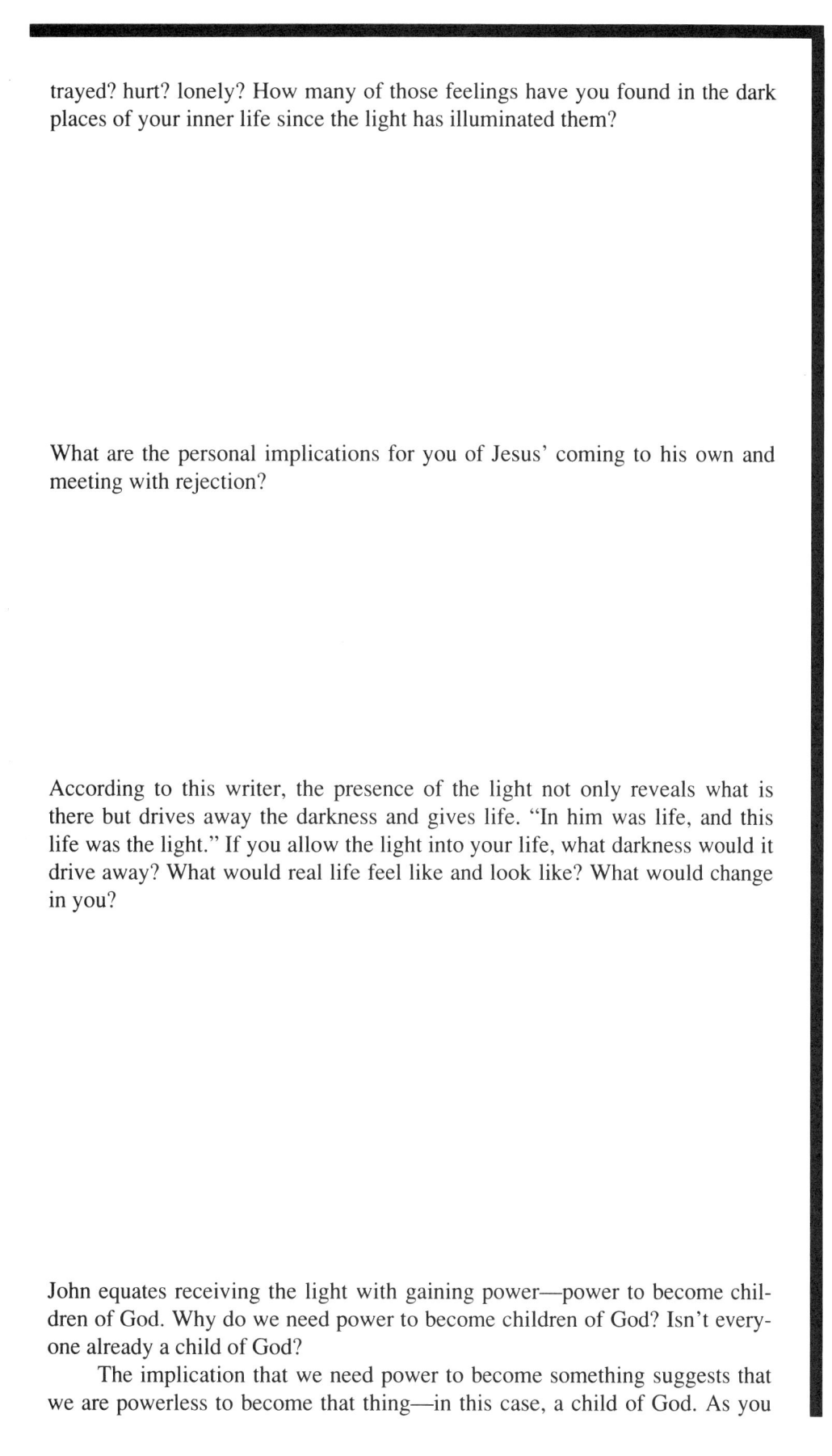

What are the personal implications for you of Jesus' coming to his own and meeting with rejection?

According to this writer, the presence of the light not only reveals what is there but drives away the darkness and gives life. "In him was life, and this life was the light." If you allow the light into your life, what darkness would it drive away? What would real life feel like and look like? What would change in you?

John equates receiving the light with gaining power—power to become children of God. Why do we need power to become children of God? Isn't everyone already a child of God?

The implication that we need power to become something suggests that we are powerless to become that thing—in this case, a child of God. As you look inward, where do you see yourself as powerless, and what are the consequences of this powerlessness? Where do you need power to become a child of God?

Close with silent meditation upon the power of God. Be still, soaking up the rays of light that overcome the darkness.

Living out of the Text

Look for two things today: Where in your community, workplace, or family do you see darkness that needs to be invaded by the true light's coming into the world? Where do you observe powerlessness in other persons or situations around you, persons that need power to become children of God? Begin to reflect on how you may be the means through which the light and life-giving Word may enter that person or situation. You may want to extend this opportunity to your church or faith community. How can you as a community of the Word become the means through which the Word gains admittance to the dark nights around you?

❋ ❋ ❋ ❋ ❋

Today is the last Sunday of Advent, though the season itself extends until Christmas Day. As you light the last Advent candle, either at worship or at home in your personal or family observance, think about your solidarity with all Christians everywhere in the world who are also giving witness to the light that is coming into the world.

DAY 23

I AM THE BREAD OF LIFE

Preparation

Saint Jerome was the fourth-century church father who translated the Bible from Greek into Latin. His version, the Vulgate, so called because it rendered the scriptures into the "vulgar" (common) language, was the principal Bible of the church until Luther made another "vulgar" translation into German during the sixteenth century. Jerome's prayer is full of scriptural imagery, which is not surprising for someone who spent so much time with the sacred texts. Let the power of this imagery center your mind and heart as you begin today.

> *Show unto me, O Lord, thy mercy,*
> *And delight my heart with it.*
> *Let me find thee,*
> *Whom I so longingly seek.*
>
> *See: here is the man*
> *Whom the robbers seized, and mishandled,*
> *And left half dead*
> *On the road to Jericho.*
> *O thou who can*
> *What the kindhearted Samaritan cannot:*
> *Come to my aid!*
>
> *I am the sheep*
> *Who wandered into the wilderness:*
> *Seek after me,*
> *And bring me home again to thy fold.*
> *Do with me what thou wilt,*
> *That all the days of my life*
> *I may bide by thee, and praise thee,*
> *With all those who art in Heaven with thee*
> *For all of eternity. Amen.*

Scripture: Read John 6:25-40.

The Gospel of John presents Jesus' acts, particularly those that are miraculous, as "signs" that point to Jesus' identity. Yet, coexisting with this emphasis on the sign-value of Jesus' actions, are certain statements—usually made by Jesus himself—that warn against looking for signs. This passage gives us an example of that tension.

In the first part of chapter 6, we find the story of the multiplication of the loaves and fish to feed a great company of people. In verse 14, the narrator says, "When the people saw the sign that he had done, they began to say, 'This is indeed the prophet who is to come into the world.'" In our passage today, we find Jesus upbraiding those who are seeking another sign from him; he tells them that he himself is the only sign they need. (See 6:35-40.)

Scholars have put forward several explanations for this tension. The two most plausible differ but are not mutually exclusive. One is that the positive sign value attached to Jesus' deeds was part of the source used by the final author or editor of the Gospel. Probably John used a separate written collection of stories of Jesus' miraculous "signs" as the basis for his project. Then John or the final editor of the Gospel introduced a somewhat less enthusiastic view of the sign value of the miracles by having Jesus downplay their significance.

The second explanation, which is not incompatible with the first, is that the tension between the positive sign value attached to the miracles and the downplaying of that value at certain points is a literary technique designed to focus the reader's attention on the person of Jesus as the reader encounters Jesus through the text. Signs are only important to the extent that they direct the witness's attention away from the signs themselves to Jesus, who is the Sign of the One who sent him. If the signs are sought for themselves, they simply become idols.

Living into the Text

The crowds who witnessed and benefited from Jesus' multiplication of the loaves and fish have followed him around the Sea of Galilee. When they catch up with him, Jesus upbraids them for being more interested in the bread that filled their stomachs than in "the food that endures for eternal life." In what ways does this story model your relationship to God? What is your motive in wanting a relationship with God? Why do you pray? What do you want besides the relationship itself? In what ways is prayer a means of getting something you want? In what ways is it a means to grow in love and converse in love with God? One way to get at these questions is to make a list of what you pray for most frequently, as well as the occasions on which you pray.

The crowd responds to Jesus' rebuke with a question: "What must we do to perform the works of God?" Jesus replies, "This is the work of God, that you believe in him whom he has sent." Follow John's spiritual equation in this passage. Working for the food that endures for eternal life = performing the works of God = believing in the one whom God has sent = eating the true bread that comes down from heaven = never hungering or thirsting again = being raised up on the last day = seeing the Son and believing = having eternal life. Whew! Talk about going round in circles! And yet, there is a profound truth here. Spend some time with John's spiritual equation. What does it mean to you to hear Jesus say, "I am the bread of life"? In what ways do you hear that statement differently now? Try to be as specific as you can in answering the question.

What does believing in Jesus as the one whom God has sent involve? Is John speaking here of an intellectual assent to a theological doctrine? Or is he talking about belief in the more personal sense of commitment to someone? If it is the second, what are the implications for your own life? What would it mean to be committed to Jesus? Be specific and concrete in your answer.

Take a few moments and pray for the needs of friends or family members that are on your heart. As you remember the needs of others, remember also your own need to believe in Christ. Pray the prayer of the man in the Gospel who cried out to Jesus, "I believe; help my unbelief."

Living out of the Text

As you go about your day, look for things that have sign value in pointing you to God. Are they things that attract attention to themselves and create desire for themselves. Or do they really point away from themselves to God? How important are these "signs" to you? In what ways are any becoming an idol to you? How are other people "signs"?

DAY 24

I AM THE LIGHT OF THE WORLD

Preparation

Bridgid of Ulster, a Celtic Christian woman of the fourth century, is remembered for her life of simplicity and charity. In this prayer, she imagines a party in her house at which Jesus and the heavenly company are gathered around her hearth making merry. Let the earthiness and homeliness of the prayer ground you in your own ordinary life so that you can open up the hearth of your heart for the friends of heaven.

> *I would like the angels of Heaven to be amongst us.*
> *I would like the abundance of peace.*
>
> *I would like full vessels of charity.*
> *I would like rich treasures of mercy.*
> *I would like cheerfulness to preside over all.*
>
> *I would like Jesus to be present.*
> *I would like the three Marys*
> *of illustrious renown to be with us.*
> *I would like the friends of Heaven*
> *to be gathered round us from all parts.*
>
> *I would like myself to be*
> *a rent payer to the Lord;*
> *that I should suffer distress,*
> *that he would bestow*
> *a good blessing upon me.*

Scripture: Read John 8:12-20.

This passage does not follow from the story of the woman taken in adultery in 8:1-11. Most commentators agree that the story in 8:1-11 is a later addition to the Gospel since many ancient manuscripts omit it, and it does interrupt the flow of the narrative from 7:52–8:12 (7:53 appears to be a rather awkward attempt to supply a narrative transition for the woman's story). See this passage then, in the context of Jesus' teaching in the Temple and the disputes in which this embroiled him (7:14 and following). At issue is the question of Jesus' identity. Is he the messiah? Is he the expected prophet who comes to announce the end of the world? Jesus' opponents reject any attempt to proclaim him as messiah or the prophet of the last days on the grounds that "no prophet is to arise from Galilee" (7:52).

In 8:12, Jesus announces with aristocratic assurance, "I am the light of the world. Whoever follows me will never walk in darkness but will have the light of life." Suddenly, we're back to the imagery of the prologue—the imagery of light and life. This Gospel is like a kaleidoscope. One image or complex of images appears; a few turns of the crank later and up it comes again, this time in a new configuration but recognizable as the same image. The literary artist who is turning the kaleidoscope has his material well in hand. We see what he wants us to see, again and again and again.

In this passage, another recurrent image appears. It is the image of where Jesus is or where he is going or where he comes from. Where Jesus' hearers are—whether they be the Pharisees (his opponents in the story), his own disciples, disciples in John's community, or opponents/disciples in our own day—depends on their recognition of where Jesus comes from and where he is now. (See the part of the farewell discourse in chapter 14 where Jesus assures his anxious disciples that he is going to prepare a place for them so that "where I am, there you may be also," or the high priestly prayer in chapter 17 where Jesus prays that "those also, whom you have given me, may be with me where I am, to see my glory.") The connection between the "where" imagery and the "light" imagery is natural. To know where someone is, one has to be able to see. If there is no light, there is only darkness; and in the darkness, one cannot know where anyone is, not even oneself.

Living into the Text

Think back to a time in your life when you felt like you were in the darkness. You couldn't see your way clearly. You were disoriented by your circumstances and anxieties. You didn't know which way to turn. Why did that situation or event feel like darkness to you? Did light ever come? How and from where did it come?

Where is there darkness in your life right now? It may be the darkness of indecision, the darkness of moral guilt, the darkness of a great trial or sorrow, the darkness of loneliness, the darkness of old resentments or anger, or the darkness of feeling lonely and unloved. In your prayer, imagine your life as a dark room, full of furniture and other unseen objects. Now imagine a door's opening at the end of that room and a bright light shines through. Notice all the things in the room. Now the light comes into the room, clearly revealing everything. Imagine that the light is a person—Jesus. What feeling does that give you to have Jesus with you in the dark room?

In your mind's eye, envision Jesus' taking you by the hand and leading you out of the dark room into a place of light. He is taking you to be with him, where he is. What would it mean for you to be with Jesus where he is?

Spend a few more moments in silence, just holding that image of Jesus' leading you from darkness into brilliant light. Don't say any words; just bask in the light.

Living out of the Text

As you meet people today, try to become sensitive to the darkness they may be experiencing. Do you hear anger in a voice? Do you sense hurt or pain? loneliness or fear? In your contact with them, imagine yourself as the one who brings them light to help them see. How will you *be* light for them?

DAY 25

I AM THE GOOD SHEPHERD

Preparation

Again, let the warmth and common beauty of Bridgid of Ulster's prayer usher you into God's waiting presence. Join her in imagining yourself as a "storehouse of bright testimony" that God wishes to bless. Meditate on what you have in your storehouse that you would like the Lord to bless.

> *O my Sovereign Lord: thou who dost give increase to all things: Bless, O God of unbounded greatness, this storehouse with thy right hand.*
>
> *My storehouse shall be a storehouse of bright testimony, the storehouse which my King shall bless, a storehouse in which plenty shall abound.*
>
> *The Son of Mary, my beloved One, will bless my storehouse. His is the glory of the whole universe. May that glory ever be multiplied, and be given unto him.*

Scripture: Read John 10:1-18.

This passage contains some confusion of images, yet the point is clear enough. In verse 2, the shepherd enters by the gate rather than climbing over the fence like a thief or robber. In verse 7, however, Jesus refers to himself as "the gate for the sheep." In verse 11, Jesus again returns to the image of himself as the "good shepherd." Is Jesus gate or shepherd? Who are the thieves and robbers? Who is the wolf?

To answer the latter questions first, we simply don't know who, if anyone, John intended to identify as the thieves or the wolf. Here he does not name the Pharisees, who are cast as the opponents earlier. Perhaps they were opponents of the Johannine community who were well-known to the members of the community but unknown to us. Or the images may not refer to any real person or persons. They simply may be literary foils for the good shepherd.

But is Jesus gate or shepherd? Perhaps the best answer is that Jesus is both. If, as is likely, John draws this imagery from real life, the shepherd was often the gate or door of the sheepfold. When the sheep were

112

safely enclosed in the fold for the night, the shepherd would lie down across the doorway and—with his own body—block the entrance of the fold to any thief or marauding wolf.

The point is that Jesus cares for his sheep enough to give his own life in sacrifice for them if need be. Interesting questions arise from verse 16. Who are the "other sheep"? What fold are they from if not from "this fold"? Which fold is "this fold"—Israel? John's community? the church in general?

Living into the Text

The image of the good shepherd is one of the most beloved of all images of Christ. It has inspired artists to paint their vision of this image. Musicians have composed hymns and anthems about the Good Shepherd. Even in an urban culture, far removed from its pastoral roots, this image still has power. The image of Christ as a shepherd didn't come to John from nowhere. He, as well as Jesus, was steeped in the imagery, particularly the scriptural imagery of his own time. Surely the beloved Psalm 23 provided some of his inspiration.

What does this image mean to you personally? What power does this image have for you? In what ways do you feel the need of a shepherd who promises security and loving care? How do you envision that care coming to you? How does the image of Jesus as the Good Shepherd translate into security where you now are aware of insecurity?

Where in your life do you feel most insecure? Where do you feel most wounded or lost? Be as specific as possible in identifying areas where you need a shepherd's care.

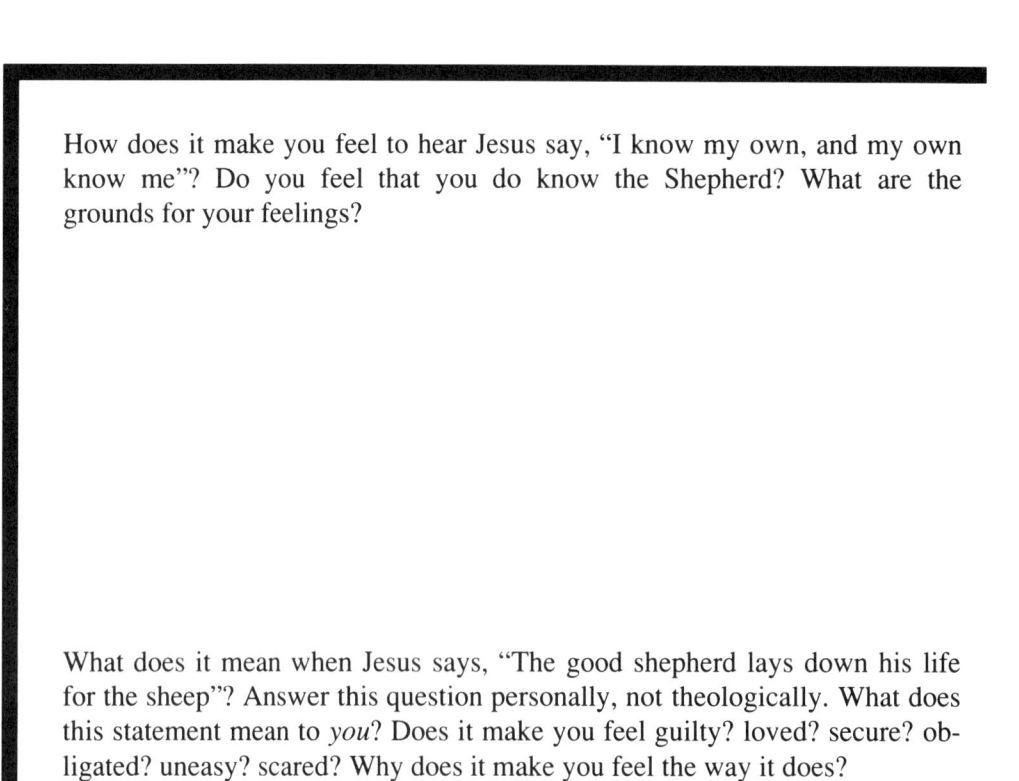

How does it make you feel to hear Jesus say, "I know my own, and my own know me"? Do you feel that you do know the Shepherd? What are the grounds for your feelings?

What does it mean when Jesus says, "The good shepherd lays down his life for the sheep"? Answer this question personally, not theologically. What does this statement mean to *you*? Does it make you feel guilty? loved? secure? obligated? uneasy? scared? Why does it make you feel the way it does?

Close your time of meditation by praying aloud Psalm 23. As much as you are able, surrender yourself to the care of the Good Shepherd.

Living out of the Text

Try to identify some of the "other sheep that do not belong to this fold." Who in your world fits this description? If the Good Shepherd wants to bring these "other sheep" into the fold, how do you see that happening? What is your part in helping it to happen?

DAY 26

I AM THE RESURRECTION AND THE LIFE

Preparation

For the remaining days in this study, we will use prayers of one of the greatest theologians and pastors of the early church, Saint Augustine. Some of Augustine's views and theology are not easily swallowed by modern Christians, particularly his negative images of sexuality, marriage, and women. He was, like all of us are, a person of his own times. However, there have been few intellectual and spiritual giants of his stature in the long history of Christian faith. His prayers have become spiritual classics, particularly his *Confessions*. In these prayers, a portrait of a passionate lover of God emerges. It is that passion for God, which above all else, commends Augustine to us as a model for our own prayer.

> *Oh! that I might repose on Thee! Oh! that Thou wouldst enter into my heart, and inebriate it, that I may forget my ills, and embrace Thee, my sole good. What art Thou to me? In Thy pity, teach me to utter it. Or what am I to Thee that Thou demandest my love, and, if I give it not, are wroth with me, and threatenest me with grievous woes? Is it then a slight woe to love Thee not? Oh! for Thy mercies' sake, tell me, O Lord my God, what Thou art unto me.* Say unto my soul, I am thy salvation. *So speak, that I may hear. Behold, Lord, my heart is before Thee; open Thou the ears thereof, and* say unto my soul, I am thy salvation. *After this voice let me haste, and take hold on Thee. Hide not Thy face from me. Let me die—lest I die—only let me see Thy face.* (Book I, 5)

Scripture: Read John 11:1-44.

Though this passage is long, few stories in the New Testament are more beautiful or touching. In John's Gospel, Jesus' raising of Lazarus, rather than his driving out the moneychangers from the Temple, provokes the authorities into arresting him. According to John, it is the religious establishment's fear of Roman reprisals against what might be perceived as a political insurrection that leads to Jesus' condemnation.

Though the story itself is the story of a miracle—the raising of a dead man to life, the portrayal of Jesus is one of the most profoundly human in any of the Gospels. Evidence[1] suggests that John has worked the story over carefully so that it fits into his theology of Jesus' miraculous deeds as "signs," which point to his true identity as the messiah. This "sign" is the climax of all the signs and prefigures Jesus' glorification, as verse 4 makes clear.

Only in John's interpretation of the story in this manner would verses 5-6 make sense, *"Accordingly, though Jesus loved Martha and her sister and Lazarus, after having heard that Lazarus was ill, he stayed two days longer in the place where he was."* Jesus' statement "I am the resurrection and the life. Those who believe in me, even though they die, will live" followed by his question to Martha, "Do you believe this?" leads to the key point John wants to make. Martha's answer (verse 27) is the central confession of one who has read the "signs" accurately: "Yes, Lord, I believe that you are the Messiah, the Son of God, the one coming into the world." With those last six words, the kaleidoscope turns, and we return to the prologue of the Gospel: "The true light, which enlightens everyone, was coming into the world" (1:9).

Living into the Text

Does Martha and Mary's reproach of Jesus, "Lord, if you had been here, my brother would not have died" (11:21, 32), ring true in your own experience? At what painful time in your life did you feel that God was absent, that God wasn't there for you? How did you feel then? angry? scared? confused? hurt? Were you able, at the time, to recognize and own those feelings? Are you able to own them now? Can you tell God exactly how you felt when the bottom fell out, and God didn't seem to be there to prevent it? To help you get in touch with those feelings, use your journal and write about them.

What does Jesus' reaction to Mary's reproach (verses 32-35) tell you about where God was when you were in pain and couldn't sense God's presence?

Another way "in" to this story as a resource for spiritual growth is to see Lazarus as a metaphor for your own life. Perhaps you can imagine yourself as "bound and wrapped" mummy-like in some destructive and death-producing behavior or emotional patterns. Can you name those binding habits of behavior, mood, or emotional patterns? If you can identify such binding forces at work in your life, imagine yourself in the grip of those forces, then hearing a voice that penetrates the darkness, "Lazarus, come out!" What is your reaction to that commanding voice?

Lazarus obeyed and came out, but it was not he who freed himself from his own bindings. Others obeyed Jesus' command to unbind Lazarus and let him go free. What does this say to you about how our liberation from the things that bind us takes place? Are you trying to free yourself? Or are you part of a community of discipline and accountability where you must depend on others to aid you in breaking free of the things that bind you? The various Twelve-Step programs such as Alcoholics Anonymous or Narcotics Anonymous take our need for such community discipline and accountability seriously. How is the church such a community?

117

What would it mean for you personally to experience Jesus as "the resurrection and the life"?

Close your time today by sitting in silence for several moments while you offer up your "graveclothes" (KJV) to the Lord and open yourself to the gift of new life.

Living out of the Text

Begin to look around for another person or a group of persons who could become a community of love and accountability for you. Who could you trust to "unbind" you in love? Christian faith can never grow if it is totally private. It can only grow in community. Begin looking for your community. In a small, intimate group, trust can develop.

---

[1] See Robert Fortna's discussion in *The Fourth Gospel and Its Predecessor*, 96ff.

DAY 27

I AM THE WAY, THE TRUTH, AND THE LIFE

Preparation

This excerpt from Augustine's *Confessions* is a refreshingly honest and heartfelt assessment of the secrecy with which even the most committed believers often cloak their motives and attitudes. Let it serve as a model for your own truth telling during Advent.

> *Narrow is the mansion of my soul; enlarge Thou it, that Thou mayest enter in. It is ruinous; repair Thou it. It has that within which must offend Thine eyes; I confess and know it. But who shall cleanse it? or to whom should I cry, save Thee?* Lord, cleanse me from my secret faults, and spare Thy servant from the power of the enemy. I believe, and therefore do I speak. *Lord, Thou knowest.* Have I not confessed against myself my transgressions unto Thee, and Thou, my God, hast forgiven the iniquity of my heart? I contend not in judgment with Thee, *who art the truth; I fear to deceive myself;* lest mine iniquity lie unto itself. *Therefore I contend not in judgment with Thee;* for if Thou, Lord, shouldst mark iniquities, O Lord, who shall abide it? (Book I, 6)

Scripture: Read John 14:1-7.

Set within the "farewell discourses" of Jesus to his disciples, this passage echoes many of the themes that recur throughout the Gospel. John equates belief in Jesus with belief in God. The theme of "going away" occurs for the second time. (See 8:21; 14:28; 16:7.) The question of "where" Jesus is reappears, connected with the theme of his "going away." The matter of knowing who Jesus is (see 1:10; 3:2; and 7:27, to name only a few) directly connects with knowing where he is going. If, as seems likely, John wrote this Gospel for second- and third-generation Christians who did not have access to the testimony of eyewitnesses of Jesus, this question of "knowing" is a poignant, personal question. How can they be certain that the message about Jesus is true? How can they know their own faith in Jesus is well-grounded? Thomas is the spokesman for this audience; his question is almost a lament. Certainly it is *the* question that the audience of this Gospel is asking: "Lord, we do not know where you are going. How can we know the way?"

Jesus' reply has often been the source of controversy in the church. In some quarters its exclusionary and ultimate character has been the main focus. In other words, persons have placed the emphasis on "No one comes to the Father except through me." There is no other way, no other truth, no other life outside of Jesus; all other quests for God are condemned as inferior at best and positively damning at worst.

Yet while we may admit the finality and ultimacy of this claim, the context appears to demand a more pastoral interpretation. Jesus makes the statement in response to a personal cry of anguish and distress on the part of one of his own disciples. It is therefore a statement meant to reassure, not to exclude. It is as though Jesus is saying to Thomas (and to the audience of the Gospel whom Thomas represents), "Don't be afraid. You don't have to search frantically for the way; I am the way. You don't have to fret about discerning the true from the false; I am the truth. You don't have to be anxious about finding life; I am the life." In this reading, the finality and ultimacy of the statement is an invitation to trust rather than a fence that excludes.

Living into the Text

The Gospel of John is an answer to an urgent human question: Where do we find real life? We find the three components of that question in Jesus' reply to Thomas's question. The way to life, the truth about life, and the character of that life are all aspects of that one human question. What direction do I take to get there? How do I avoid taking a dead end road? and How will I know it when I find it? These are all part of the same question. Yet to answer that question for ourselves, we may need to think about each of the components separately.

What direction are you taking, or what road have you embarked upon in your own quest for real life? What road signs indicate that you will find life at the end of this road? How do you know that you have found the right way? What other roads have you embarked upon in the past, and where have those roads led?

How do you know the road you're on is the right road and not a dead end or detour? Augustine's prayer in which he confesses the falsehood in his own heart may help us here. All of us are "people of the lie," as M. Scott Peck puts it in his best-selling book by that name. We are easily confused and led astray from truth by our propensity for living in denial, for projecting our feelings and motives onto other people, for protecting ourselves from intimacy or injury. Such self-deception will never lead us to real life. Where within yourself do you see such a tendency to deceive yourself? Naming your own falsehoods is the surest way to get on the right road, the road of truth.

What is real life to you? What would it look like? How would you know it if you found it? Describe your ultimate hunger as specifically as you can. Does your present experience contain much, if any, of your vision of what real life is? How do you personally respond to Jesus' statement, "I am the way, and the truth, and the life"?

Close your time today by praying the prayer of Saint Augustine with which you began this exercise. Let it become your prayer as you seek to discover your true life in Christ.

Living out of the Text

If you have time, amid all your Christmas preparations, watch some TV, listen to the radio, or look through a magazine. Look and listen, through the advertising, for appeals that seem to promise real life but that you can identify as falsehoods. Becoming consciously aware of the lure of the false is the first step in discerning what is true.

DAY 28

I AM THE TRUE VINE

Preparation

This excerpt from Saint Augustine's *Confessions* likens God to a physician whose medicines heal the troubled soul.

> *But thou, Lord,* abidest for ever, *yet not for ever art Thou angry with us; because Thou pitiest our dust and ashes, and it was pleasing in Thy sight to reform my deformities; and by inward goads didst Thou rouse me, that I should be ill at ease, until Thou wert manifested to my inward sight. Thus, by the secret hand of Thy medicining was my swelling abated, and the troubled and bedimmed eyesight of my mind, by the smarting anointings of healthful sorrows, was from day to day healed.*
>
> *And Thou, willing first to shew me, how Thou* resistest the proud, but givest grace unto the humble, *and by how great an act of Thy mercy Thou hadst traced out to [mortals] the way of humility, in that Thy* WORD *was made flesh, and dwelt among [us].*
> (Book VII, 12 and 13)

Scripture: Read John 15:1-12.

Chapters 14–16 and the so-called high priestly prayer of chapter 17 are probably John's own additions to the earlier narrative source that underlies the narrative portions of this Gospel. We hear echoes of the situation of John's community in this "farewell discourse" of Jesus. The opening verses of chapter 16 provide one of those echoes. The reference to being "put out of the synagogues" and being killed surely describes the very situation and concerns this Gospel was written to address.

Setting it in the context of the last supper, John designs the discourse to reassure a community of people going through a painful time of separation from its own religious traditions, with consequent separations within families and between former friends. Questions from Peter (13:36) and Thomas (14:5) about where Jesus is going echo the questions of believers in John's community who know that Jesus "went away"; that is, he died. But they themselves are not firsthand witnesses of his resurrection. In a time of deep personal anguish, how can they know "where" he has gone? How can they know their present struggle is not in vain?

Jesus' answer in this discourse is that he will come again to this community of disciples through the agency of the "Spirit of truth" or "Advocate." John, unlike other early Christian thinkers, appears to have little or no expectation of a "second coming" of Christ at the end of the age. For him, Christ has come already and presently abides with his beleaguered community of disciples.

In this Gospel's context, Jesus' promise, "I will come again and will take you to myself, so that where I am, there you may be also" (14:3), probably means his return to his disciples as the Risen One through the Holy Spirit, following his "going away" on the cross. What was true for the disciples firsthand will be true for these disciples in John's community who are believers at second or thirdhand. Their experience of the risen Jesus will be every bit as real and immediate as the experience of Jesus' first disciples. Time and distance are irrelevant. They will be "where he is," and that will be enough.

Chapter 15 gives the formula for experiencing this "coming again." It is to "abide in me as I abide in you." If they will abide in Jesus as branches abide in a vine, they will experience several results: They will be able to ask whatever they will, and it will be done for them; they will bear much fruit; they will abide in Christ's love; and they will know the fullness of joy.

How does the community abide in the true vine? "If you keep my commandments, you will abide in my love. . . . This is my commandment, that you love one another as I have loved you."

Living into the Text

Mark 13 orients us toward the future, toward the end point of God's creative and redeeming purpose for the world and offers hope as the mode of living. John's farewell discourses orient us toward the present reality of the presence of Christ through the Holy Spirit in the community of faith. The operative word for disciples in the Johannine mode is *abide*.

Reflect on the imagery of a vine and its branches. Is a vine an individual entity or a community? Is a vine without branches a vine at all, and are branches anything at all without the vine? What does this reflection tell you about the nature of Christian faith?

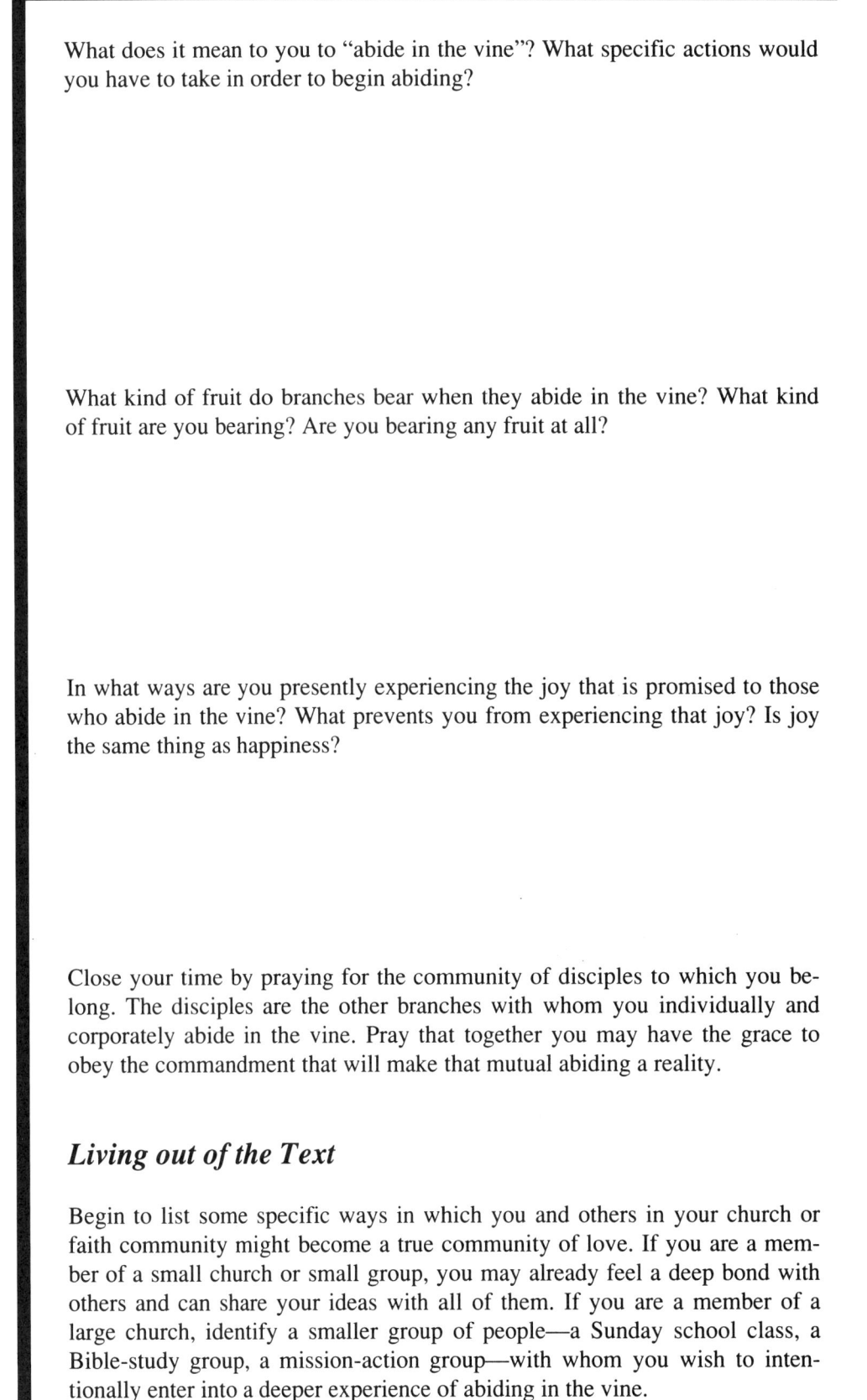

What does it mean to you to "abide in the vine"? What specific actions would you have to take in order to begin abiding?

What kind of fruit do branches bear when they abide in the vine? What kind of fruit are you bearing? Are you bearing any fruit at all?

In what ways are you presently experiencing the joy that is promised to those who abide in the vine? What prevents you from experiencing that joy? Is joy the same thing as happiness?

Close your time by praying for the community of disciples to which you belong. The disciples are the other branches with whom you individually and corporately abide in the vine. Pray that together you may have the grace to obey the commandment that will make that mutual abiding a reality.

Living out of the Text

Begin to list some specific ways in which you and others in your church or faith community might become a true community of love. If you are a member of a small church or small group, you may already feel a deep bond with others and can share your ideas with all of them. If you are a member of a large church, identify a smaller group of people—a Sunday school class, a Bible-study group, a mission-action group—with whom you wish to intentionally enter into a deeper experience of abiding in the vine.

DAY 29

THE WORD BECAME FLESH

Use this exercise on Christmas Day regardless of what day of the week it is. You may have to skip one or more exercises in this fourth week or do them after Christmas Day. Use this one on December 25.

Preparation

As part of your celebration today, pray the following portion from this ancient fourth-century liturgical prayer to be said at Christmas. It is known as the "Leonine Sacramentary" (named after Leo the Great). You may wish to have family or friends join you in praying it aloud.

> *Grant, O merciful God, that he who was born this day to be the Savior of the world, as he is the author of our divine birth, so may be himself the bestower of our immortality; through the same Jesus Christ our Lord.*
>
> *Almighty and everlasting God, who hast willed that on the nativity of our Lord Jesus Christ, thy Son, should depend the beginning and the completion of all religion; grant us, we beseech thee, to be reckoned as a portion of him, on whom is built the whole salvation of [humankind].*
>
> *We beseech thee, O Lord, bestow on thy servants the increase of faith, hope, and charity; that as they glory in the nativity of thy Son our Lord, they may, by thy governance, not feel the adversities of this world; and also that what they desire to celebrate in time, they may enjoy to all eternity; through the same Jesus Christ our Lord. . . .*
>
> *Grant unto us, we pray thee, O Lord our God, that we who rejoice to keep the feast of the nativity of Jesus Christ our Lord, may by walking worthily of him attain to fellowship with him, through the same Jesus Christ our Lord.*
>
> *Grant, O Lord, we beseech thee, to thy people an inviolable firmness of faith; that as they confess thine only-begotten Son, the everlasting partaker of thy glory, to have been born in our very flesh, of the Virgin Mother, they may be delivered from present adversities, and admitted into joys that shall abide; through the same Jesus Christ our Lord.*

Scripture: Read John 1:14-18

Because of its mystical and spiritual character, many Jewish and Christian gnostic sects who espoused a dualism between spirit (as good) and flesh (as evil) seized upon the Fourth Gospel as the favorite Gospel almost as soon as it was written. Those who operated out of this dualism favored a Jesus who was never quite a human being of flesh and blood but always a thinly disguised divinity who wore the appearance of humanity.

Yet the Fourth Evangelist will not be co-opted so easily. It is hard to imagine a more devastating refutation of such notions or to imagine a more pointed statement of what we have come to call the Incarnation: "And the Word became flesh and lived among us, and we have seen his glory, the glory as of a father's only son, full of grace and truth." The purpose of the Fourth Gospel is to help its audience—believers of whatever generation, who must depend on the testimony of others—to see the glory of the Eternal Word in the face of a flesh-and-blood person like ourselves.

Living into the Text

We are now at the end of our journey through Advent. The inward-looking sense of expectation of this season gives way to joyous celebration of God's "indescribable gift" (2 Corinthians 9:15). As a way of giving this celebration some concrete focus, try to describe what the phrase "The Word became flesh" means to you personally. What personal experience(s) of the Incarnation have you had? What difference does it make to you personally that Jesus was a human being in the fullest sense of the word?

John says, "From his fullness we have all received, grace upon grace." What piling up of grace (free and abundant gift) have you received? Can you accept that in Christ we do receive "grace upon grace"? If not, what is preventing your acceptance?

"No one has ever seen God. It is God the only Son, who is close to the Father's heart, who has made him known." The Christian has only one answer to the question, "What is God like?" God is like Jesus. To celebrate this truth, draw your own portrait of God. Describe what God is like for you. Use words, images, or even colors and sounds to "draw" your portrait of God.

Close your time today by singing the second stanza of Charles Wesley's great hymn to the Incarnation, "Hark! the Herald Angels Sing."

> *Christ, by highest heaven adored;*
> *Christ, the everlasting Lord;*
> *Late in time, behold him come,*
> *offspring of a virgin's womb.*
> *Veiled in flesh the Godhead see;*
> *hail th' incarnate Deity,*
> *pleased with us in flesh to dwell,*
> *Jesus, our Emmanuel.*

Living out of the Text

Remember that though our Advent journey has reached its goal, the journey of growing in Christ never ends. It is a journey that will take us through this life and the next, a road that takes us ever deeper into that love that came down at Christmas until, as Charles Wesley put it, we are "lost in wonder, love, and praise."

WEEK FOUR

Group Meeting

Gathering

Spend a few moments in casual conversation. Sharing Christmas experiences is an appropriate topic. Ask how the others celebrate the holiday. Share some of your own traditions.

Sharing the Journey

1. Share highlights of the fourth week's exercises. Which did you find most meaningful and why?

2. Encourage persons to express their reactions to the very different quality of John's Gospel when compared with the other three Gospels. Consider these questions:

   In what ways is John's Gospel more mystical and spiritual interpretation of Jesus to your liking?

   What gave you difficulty in John's Gospel?

3. Reflect on how our Christmas celebration would differ if we only had John 1:1-18, without the birth stories in Matthew and Luke.

4. Look back over the whole Advent journey. What parts of the journey did you find most meaningful?

5. Suggest the possibility of continuing as a group to maintain the important elements of mutual encouragement and accountability. You may wish to follow the lectionary readings or some other plan of scripture reading. Many Bible-study helps are available, but the Bible itself, a good Bible dictionary, and a good one-volume Bible commentary will take you a long way.

Closing

Celebrate your journey together by singing some favorite Christmas carols.